If you thought vegan food was brown and bland, think again.

V *is for Vegan* is the cookbook that blows that myth out of the water. Kerstin Rodgers' 150 recipes are game-changing, with easy ideas for flavour bombs like home-made vegan parmesan and pesto, breakfast treats, stunning soups and salads, dips, snacks, condiments and spice mixes, naturally vegan dinners, and desserts you never thought possible without eggs or dairy.

This is the essential book for anyone who's ever thought about cutting down their meat or dairy intake, who's already vegan or vegetarian and wants to cook imaginative dishes, and for people who simply love great-tasting food. Creative, unique and packed with tips and advice, V *is for Vegan* will change the way you think about vegan cooking.

V

is for vegan

KERSTIN RODGERS
aka MsMarmiteLover

Photography by Jan Baldwin

Quadrille
PUBLISHING

Unusual Ingredients

Contents

Introduction

What Do Vegans Eat?

This is the question most people ask. It is a plant-based diet.

In other words, if no animals were used in the ingredients of the dish, it's vegan.

Is It Easy?

The truth is that a vegan or vegetarian cook works harder.

There is more prep with vegetables than any other foodstuff. Think of the scrubbing, peeling, chopping and blanching.

Although there are quick, simple dishes in this book, for the intrepid cook who wants to stretch their capabilities and expand their repertoire, there are also more complicated recipes.

The vegan cook must also work on flavour. There is no instant umami (savoury) flavour coming from the Maillard (browning) reactions of seared flesh. But you can accomplish these flavour boosts in vegan cooking too. The vegan cook also draws on food from around the world to provide variety. The vegan cook is adventurous with ingredients.

Homely Food, Simply Cooked?

While I'm a great believer in simplicity, letting the ingredient take centre stage, some vegans use complex cooking techniques to prepare their dishes. With the effort it takes to become vegan, most vegans spend time preparing their meals. This means that they will research and discover cutting-edge food preparation and rediscover old forgotten techniques.

Substitutes

Vegans use substitutes to replace animal products. In this book you will find recipes to make your own vegan substitutes for milk, butter, cheese, yoghurt and mayonnaise. As a cook I don't go for mock meats such as TVP (Textured Vegetable Protein) or 'facon' (fake bacon). I prefer to use natural, unprocessed foods.

What Vegans Don't Eat & Why

"The greatness of a nation and its moral progress can be judged by the way its animals are treated."
Mahatma Gandhi

Vegans have two primary objections to eating animal-derived food: ethical and environmental. For the former, some people simply feel uncomfortable eating sentient food and have strong feelings about animal welfare. For the latter, industrial livestock farming is undeniably having a disastrous effect on the environment. Most modern farming is industrial. Only a tiny proportion of animals are reared on a traditional farm.

So even if you don't become a full-time vegan, lowering your industrial meat and farmed fish intake is good for you, good for the planet and good for animals. The only direct power we have is as consumers, so unless you know the source of your animal product, don't buy it.

Here is some information if you are thinking of going vegan for ethical reasons. No dogma, no guilt trip, just some information to think about.

Meat

We never used to eat this much flesh: meat eating has gone up by 300% over the last 50 years. Yet the price of meat and fish as a proportion of our income has plummeted. This can only be achieved by treating industrially farmed animals very badly.

Cattle need water, feed and land. Our beef addiction destroys rainforests. As Dr Mark Post, scientist and creator of synthetic lab meat, comments, "It takes 100g of plant food to create 15g of meat; this isn't an efficient use of our resources."

Not only do industrially farmed livestock have terrible lives, it affects our environment. One instance: pig manure from industrial farming is on such a scale that it is leaking into the water table. People that live near these factory farms have asthma and other health problems.

Over the last few decades, there have been endless scandals regarding the cheap meat available in our shops, from Mad Cow Disease to the horse meat scandal. Meat eaters have no idea what they are eating.

Dairy

Consuming dairy, you might think, does not harm animals. But the dairy industry, under the system of intensive factory farming, is cruel. Cows left to their own devices live, on average, to be 20 years old, but industrial dairy cows live a mere 4 or 5 years. Cows are kept constantly pregnant and lactating, and given hormones to grow to adolescence more quickly. The milking machines cause pain and injury. The tiny baby bulls are removed from their mothers within one day of being born and are kept in the dark, then killed as veal, while the calves are removed at one day old and fed milk replacers. Baby cows don't get the milk; we do. But that milk often contains pesticides, pus, hormones and antibiotics.

Eggs

Only female chickens produce eggs, so in industrial egg production the males are disposed of, often while still alive. All industrial egg production, even if 'free range', is cruel. The hens are kept in crowded conditions, their beaks are amputated, they are pushed to produce more eggs than is natural, which deprives their bodies of calcium, and as soon as their egg production goes down, they are killed.

Fish

Problems include over-fishing, to the point that many species (cod, tuna) will be extinct within 50 years. Farmed fish eat their own body weight in antibiotics to combat disease from overcrowding. Dredge-net fishing, using nets the size of several football fields, is a crude commercial way of fishing, killing dolphins and sea turtles (by-catch) along with the fish. Radiation is also a problem, due to the Fukushima nuclear disaster.

Jelly

Jelly and gelatine are made from cows' hooves. Vegan, plant-based alternatives (carrageen, agar agar) are available but so far do not have all the qualities of jelly, which melts at body temperature.

Honey

Most honey comes from farmed bees and, just like other industrially farmed creatures, they are mistreated. Their hives are artificially fed with sugar or corn syrup rather than nectar, so their honey is of poor quality. Bee numbers are declining because of pesticides, antibiotics, being restricted to the nectar of monoculture crops and mobile phones messing with their navigation systems. If you buy honey, find out about natural beekeeping, which respects the hive.

Finally, each bee produces about a teaspoon of honey during its lifetime. Bees produce honey because they need it, to survive winter.

Alcohol?

There are vegan wines, beer or 'natural' wines. But wine doesn't have animal products in it, I hear you say. Actually, egg whites, fish bladders, albumen, milk protein and shellfish are used for clarification. Most 'natural' wines (which contain no additives or sulphur) are vegan. Most hard alcohol is vegan.

Vegan Cosmetics & Clothes

Dedicated vegans use vegan-friendly cosmetics, nail varnish, shampoo and conditioner. Pearlised eyeshadow is created from oyster shells.

Some vegans will also avoid medicines that contain animal products; however, all medicines are currently tested on animals prior to being used by humans.

Strict vegans do not wear leather, fur, wool, ivory or bone jewellery, silk (made from silkworms boiled alive), feathers or pearls. Pearls used to be very rare, but nowadays are farmed industrially.

Brief History of Veganism

Veganism is not a newfangled thing. In Ancient Greece, philosophers such as Pythagoras argued that both humans and animals should be treated with respect. By the late 4th century BC, a debate had developed between two opposing schools of thought: while Theophrastus suggested that animals possess reason, Aristotle disagreed.

Around the time of Jesus Christ, many sects discussed the mistreatment of other species. There is a long tradition of people refusing to eat animal-derived foods based on either religion or philosophy. Many devout Christians

assert that Jesus was a vegetarian, and cite the commandment 'Thou shalt not kill' and the Book of Daniel.

Centuries later, in the UK, anti-monarchist Oliver Cromwell passed animal welfare laws (1653) and Puritanism became associated with animal protection.

During the French enlightenment, humanist philosopher Rousseau argued in *A Discourse on Inequality* (1755) that animals are sentient beings. Later he encouraged a vegetarian diet for children.

During the early 19th century in Britain, moral discourse advocated restraint with regard to eating meat, and there was a parallel between better treatment of animals and the anti-slavery movement.

Dr William Lambe wrote the first ever vegan diet book *Water and Vegetable Diet in Consumption, Scrofula, Cancer, Asthma and Other Chronic Diseases* (1815). The early 19th century was also the romantic period, which valued compassion and nature, and poet Percy Bysshe Shelley, his wife Mary, plus their friend Byron all became vegan for periods of time. Shelley lived for a while in a vegan commune in Bracknell. He wrote *A Vindication of Natural Diet* (1813), while Mary Shelley wrote the celebrated book *Frankenstein* (1818) whose famous 'monster' is vegan! At the same time, more fruits and vegetables were available in Europe, making a meat-free diet more accessible.

In 1824 in the UK, the RSPCA was formed by anti-slavery parliamentarian William Wilberforce and others, including Lewis Gompertz who published *Moral Inquiries on the Situation of Man and of Brutes*. Gompertz was possibly the first 'freegan' – he thought that if the

animal died of natural causes, it was fine to eat meat and if a calf died naturally, it was fine to drink the milk of the mother.

In the USA, there was a similar drive towards a plant-based diet in the early to mid-19th century, for health and spiritual reasons.

Influential author, philosopher and abolitionist Henry David Thoreau ate only plant-based foods. Dr Sylvester Graham, creator of Graham (wholewheat) flour, published *Lectures on the Science of Human Life* (1839), advocating a diet of plant food and water. Bronson Alcott, father of Louisa May Alcott who wrote *Little Women*, was an advocate of the 'vegetable diet'. He opened a vegan commune in New England called Fruitlands. Alcott was also an abolitionist who argued for women's rights. Alcott then travelled to England where the first vegetarian school, Alcott House School, was opened just outside of London.

Back in the UK, William Horsell created the London Vegetarian Association (1847) and then published *Hydropathy for the People: with Plain Observations on Drugs, Diet, Water, Air, and Exercise*. Horsell's wife, Elizabeth, was also an active vegetarian and writer. When Horsell died, she went on to open a vegetarian girl's boarding school.

Three years later, The American Vegetarian Society was formed, led by Sylvester Graham and Russell Thacher Trall; the latter, a naturopathic doctor, published the first official 'vegan' cookbook (1854).

In Germany, Gustav Schlickeysen published *Fruit and Bread - A Scientific Diet* (1875), which is vegan, fruitarian and raw-foodarian.

1887: Dr Kellogg, inventor of the cornflake, was also vegan. He was a great promoter of soya products and rediscovered soya milk, used for centuries in Chinese cuisine, as part of a healthy, plant-based diet. (USA)

1886: Henry Salt, master at Eton, published *A Plea for Vegetarianism* and coined the phrase 'animal rights'. (UK)

1900: Maximilian Bircher-Benner invented Bircher muesli. He was strongly influenced by the writings of Schlickeysen. (Switzerland)

1910: The publication of the first British vegan cookbook *No Animal Food and Nutrition and Diet with Vegetable Recipes* by Rupert Wheldon.

1931: Mahatma Gandhi spoke at the London Vegetarian Society. Ghandi was influenced by the works of Thoreau and Salt.

1944: The invention of the word 'vegan': Donald Watson, a Yorkshireman, coined the term and founded the Vegan Society. Watson lived a long, healthy life, dying in 2005 at the age of 95.

Vegan Religions

Rastas
Buddhists
Some Hindus including:
Hare Krishna
Brahma Kumaris
Jain

Know Your 'egans' and Your 'arians'

Vegans: eat no animal products whatsoever.

Pescatarians: will not eat meat, red or white, but will eat fish.

Pollotarians: will not eat meat from a mammal but will eat chicken.

Freegans: a portmanteau word combining 'free' and 'vegan'; freegans do not buy animal products. This is an anti-consumerist, anti-food waste movement, so they will eat animal products if they would otherwise be discarded.

Flexitarians: are semi-vegetarian. They occasionally eat meat. These are people who are 'meat reducers', that is, trying to reduce the amount of meat they eat, or at the very least, trying to source meat from ethical suppliers. They are probably the biggest sector.

Vegetarians

Ovo-lacto-vegetarians: will eat plant foods plus eggs and dairy.

Lacto-vegetarians: will eat dairy but no eggs.

Ayurvedics: are vegan, but do not eat garlic, mushrooms or onions because these are supposed to 'excite' the body.

Raw foodists: only eat raw, uncooked food (cooked at less than 46°C), as cooked food loses many nutritional benefits. They often use sprouted or fermented foods. They sometimes eat raw fish, eggs and meat.

Fruitarians: only eat fruit, berries, seeds and nuts.

Juicearians: exist on consuming only smoothies and juices made from fruit and vegetables.

Breatharians: don't eat food, they only need sunlight and fresh air. Don't try this at home.

Knowledge is Power

A vegan diet is easier than you think. Basically, you can eat anything that is derived from plants, and it's amazing when you discover what flavours can be achieved without meat. This chapter will shed some light on the hoards of amazing ingredients and foodstuffs you can stock up on or make yourself. Armed with this knowledge, you can be bold in the kitchen. And you'll never run out of ideas for how to pep up your dinner.

Umami Flavour Bombs: The Vegan Toolkit

Here is a toolbox of 'flavour bombs' that will instantly pep up your food.

Umami Boosters

Anything preserved or fermented increases the umami (savouriness) factor in food. Some of these ingredients you will know, others may be new to you. The money you save on cutting out animal products can be put towards some of these interesting ingredients.

Mushrooms are very umami: apart from the standard ones such as button or brown, splash out from time to time on shiitake, chanterelles or morels (the latter are very expensive even in season, but they are gorgeous little cylindrical sponges of flavour). Dried mushrooms such as porcini can, when rehydrated, boost savouriness very effectively.

Huitlacoche is a Mexican fungus that grows on corn. Buy it tinned from Mexican online stockists and use a mere smear to add intense flavour.

Truffles are the most luxurious fungus you can buy. A few shavings of this in pasta or in a creamy cashew cheese gratin can transform the dish. Who says veganism isn't high class?

Marmite is a favourite ingredient of mine. Use it to flavour stews, soups and pasta, or on toast.

The best quality soy sauce tends to be Japanese and rather more expensive than Chinese. Shoyu is the Japanese name for soy sauce. Within Chinese cooking there are light and dark soy sauces; dark soy sauce contains caramel and is used for cooking, to deepen colour, while light soy is added to cooked food for enhancing flavour, almost like salt. Tamari (Japanese for 'puddle') is gluten-free: unlike soy sauce, it doesn't use wheat; rather, it is the liquid content of soya-bean miso. Alternative soy-like sauces include Maggi Liquid Seasoning (which contains the herb lovage) and Braggs Liquid Aminos. Both are delicious.

Nutritional yeast flakes are used by everyone in the vegan world and are the secret ingredient of many recipes — a good replacement for cheesy flavour. It's amazing how a few yeast flakes can transform the flavour of a dish.

Vegan 'Parmesan'

Makes a handful

3 tbsp nutritional yeast

50g pecan nuts

Pinch of sea salt

In a food processor, grind the ingredients to a coarse, crumbly powder. Add to pasta, potatoes, polenta etc.

Miso is a fermented grain paste and one of the oldest foods in Japan. It comes in light and dark forms, is red, white or brown and can be made from barley, rice, buckwheat, rye or millet. You can buy it from Japanese shops or online. Stir it into soups, spread it over grilled vegetables, whisk it into salad dressings or use as a dip.

Knowledge is Power

You may be surprised to know that chocolate is fermented. Do like the Mexicans and use it in savoury as well as sweet foods — for instance the mole on page 142.

Tomato purée is an intense umami ingredient, good for soups and pasta sauce and as a base sauce for pizza. You can make your own — a good idea if you come by a large amount of cheap tomatoes in season. Peel and deseed them, add 1 tsp salt for every 6 tomatoes and cook them on a low simmer in a heavy pot in the oven for several hours. Tomatoes are one of the few foods that have more minerals and vitamins after cooking than raw.

Liquid smoke is a cheaty way to get a smoky flavour in your food. It's particularly gorgeous with beans or tofu and it's available in many supermarkets.

Citrus

There is so much more to the world of citrus than oranges and lemons, although I do like to use the zest of these well known fruits as a last-minute reviver on many of my dishes. Zested lemon is reported to be good for its antiseptic qualities and to deter fatigue. By the way, it's the white pith that is bitter, not the yellow skin.

My latest citrus crush is **Bengali lime**, a large knobbly green fruit with floral notes which I discovered in a local Bangladeshi grocery shop. Do check ethnic shops if you live in a city. I've also made preserved lemons from tiny Indian yellow limes, found hanging mysteriously in a brightly coloured plastic net at the shop around the corner from me.

Japanese yuzu has come to the fore in the last few years. Although it's impossible at present to get fresh yuzu in the UK, you can buy the juice, the paste and ponzu, a yuzu/soy sauce. In the States they have access to Meyer lemons, also very floral. If you ever come across a kaffir lime, or indeed the plant, buy it. Not only will you have fresh kaffir lime for your Thai curries but also use of the leaves.

I've also used **kumquats**, small oval orange fruit with a sweet skin.

Grapefruit farmers are growing new, sweeter cultivars, but it's also true that bitter foods are good for you.

Pomelo is an Asian fruit, not unlike grapefruit, which I've used in the oriental-influenced salad on page 99.

Preserved Lemons, Satsumas & Limes

(Photo on page 10.)

Makes a 350ml jar

8—10 small Indian lemons (or 5—6 big lemons), limes or satsumas

250g rock salt

Juice of 5 lemons

Sterilise a 350ml jar by washing it thoroughly in hot soapy water, rinsing well and then placing it in an oven preheated to 170°C/gas mark 3 for 15 minutes. Sterilise the lid in boiling water for 15 minutes, with the rubber seal if the jar has one.

Meanwhile, wash the outside of all the citrus and cut into quarters, without cutting all the way through, so that the 4 sections are attached at one end. Pack the salt inside the fruit, leaving the filled citrus in a bowl until the jar is ready.

Put a 5mm layer of salt in the bottom of the hot, sterilised jar, then carefully fill with the salt-stuffed citrus, sprinkling a little salt between the layers. Press down once you have filled the jar and top up with the lemon juice, and some water if necessary, to cover the fruit. Close the jar and keep an eye on it for the next 3 or 4 days, making sure that the level of liquid does not dip below the fruit. Then, once you are confident that the fruit will remain submerged, store for 6 weeks in a cool, dark place before using it, finely sliced and added to grain dishes.

Useful Spices

I mention these spices, as you may not be aware of just how fab they are. Do regularly inspect and chuck spices — out-of-date ones are worse than useless, tasting like old moths. Keep them in a cool, dark place.

Achiote is like the Mexican version of saffron and hard to describe! Apart from adding a deep rusty colour, it also imparts a kind of savoury muddy clay flavour. It's good, I promise.

Saffron is one of the most expensive spices in the world, made from crocus stamens. A mere pinch adds new depth to any dish. I make saffron and tomato spaghetti sauce, lifting this classic, well known dish above the ordinary (see page 126).

Ras el hanout is Arabic for something approximating 'the best of the shop'. Every family has its own version, but it's a ground mixture of spice and rose petals. It can be bought at most supermarkets nowadays, so add it to dips and North African/Arabic dishes.

Sumac is a citrussy berry, very popular in Middle Eastern cookery. Nowadays it is widely available. Sprinkle ground sumac over roast vegetables, pumpkin and squash, and dips.

Chinese five-spice contains Sichuan pepper, cloves, cinnamon, fennel seeds and star anise, and is good in stir-fries and on tofu.

Japanese seven-spice or **shichimi** is a blend of chilli, orange peel, black and white sesame seeds, hemp seeds, ground ginger, nori and sansho.

Black limes are dried limes often used in Persian cooking. Crumble them into bean dishes or rice to add a sour flavour.

Sweet smoked paprika, especially the Spanish kind called pimentón de la Vera, instantly gives depth to any dish — some say it even tastes a bit like bacon. Hungarian paprika, however, retains its red colour during cooking.

Pickled & Preserved Flavour Intensifiers

I love sweet and salty together, and most pickles require acidity too, to create an 'agrodolce' zing to your food. Olives, capers, pickled peppercorns and preserved plums can be bought in jars to augment and counterpoint. Chutneys and atchars perform the same function, adding a flavour focus to Indian food. Pickling can be done in vinegar or in brine. Traditional brining gives pickles probiotic qualities and are good for your health.

Pink Pickled Onions

These can be made in half an hour, are very pretty and can be used in salads, sandwiches or burgers as a relish. I love them so much that I eat them out of the jar and have to make more. (Photo on page 10.)

Makes a 500ml jar

150ml red wine vinegar

3 tbsp sea salt

2 tbsp caster sugar

250ml water

1 large red onion, finely sliced

Mix the vinegar, salt, sugar and water, stirring to dissolve the sugar and salt. Put the onion in a sterilised 500ml jar (see page 13), top with as much pickling liquid as will fit and leave for 30 minutes or so and it will turn a hot pink colour. Eat within 2 weeks.

Pickled Green Grapes

I used 'sultana' grapes from my local shop which stocks Turkish food, but you can use any seedless white/green grapes. I keep a jar of these in my larder and sling them on salads. (Photo on page 10.)

Makes a 500ml jar

150ml white wine vinegar

2 tbsp caster sugar

3 tbsp coarse sea salt or sel gris

1 tbsp mustard seeds

250ml water

250g seedless green grapes (only unbruised fruit), stems removed

Mix the vinegar, sugar, salt, mustard seeds and water together in a medium saucepan and heat until the sugar has dissolved, then remove from the heat and let it cool. Put the grapes in a sterilised 500ml jar (see page 13) and top with as much cool pickling liquid as will fit. These will keep for months.

A salsa is made of finely chopped vegetables and fruit, dressed with lemon or lime and seasoned. It is fine enough to serve as a sauce. A classic salsa contains tomatoes, onion, jalapeño, lime and coriander. Mexican pico de gallo is very similar to salsa, with almost identical ingredients, but it is less liquid and chunkier. Make an unusual salsa by dicing and mixing mango, spring onion and fresh ginger together and seasoning with salt.

A kachumber is a finely diced piquant salad found in Indian cookery. It is very similar to Mexican salsa but with the addition of spices such as cumin, coriander, paprika and chaat masala.

Chimichurri is an Argentinian relish made from parsley, garlic, olive oil, oregano, white wine vinegar and salt, all minced together.

Sambal is a southern Indian version of a kachumber, but it is sometimes a paste; a coconut, lime and chilli recipe for this is on page 82.

Oils

I like to use different oils, not just the standard olive oil for dressings, and vegetable or sunflower oil for frying.

Olive oil has a distinct flavour and the best quality should be used on food, as heating it will destroy some of its quality. Extra virgin olive oil is new oil — that is what is meant by 'virgin'. It shouldn't have any mustiness or mould in the scent; it should taste and smell grassy, peppery, vital.

Sunflower oil in the UK is regarded as a bog-standard cooking oil, but when I visited Georgia, it was dark kelp in colour, with an intense flavour. You could just dip your bread in it, like we do with olive oil.

Austria has a rich pumpkin seed oil that is worth trying.

Sometimes you want a neutral oil for a dish: Asian cooking uses groundnut oil for this purpose, with sesame oil as a finishing touch.

I also use **walnut, hazelnut, avocado, macadamia, coconut, mustard** or **hay-smoked rapeseed oil.**

Do experiment with oils and vinegars, adding herbs, chilli and citrus, to introduce yet another element to plant-based cookery. Store oil in a cool, dark place; I once mistakenly kept a 5-litre can of good olive oil next to my Aga for a couple of days and the next time I used it I ruined a whole recipe, as it was disgustingly rancid.

Nuts, Seeds & Herbs

You will be using nuts and seeds as a protein substitute for animal products. A few lightly toasted nuts and seeds are a tasty, textural garnish on salads and soups; I sling them in everything.

Nut milks are useful and quick to make. In fact, once you've made your own, you'll wonder why cows' milk is still the standard.

Dukkah is an Egyptian nut and herb mix: try it as a snack with bread and oil, or sprinkle it over dishes.

Macadamia Dukkah

Makes a small bowlful

100g macadamia nuts

1 tsp coriander seeds

½ tsp cumin seeds

2 tbsp za'atar (a Middle Eastern
  herb mix with thyme)

1 tsp dried mint

Sea salt

Dry-roast the nuts and seeds in separate batches in a frying pan over a medium-high heat. Let cool, then blitz with the za'atar and mint using a food processor or pestle and mortar until crumbly. Salt to taste.

Gomashio is a dry Japanese condiment. Make your own by roasting 50g black sesame seeds and then grinding with 1 tsp sea salt.

An Italian herby condiment, **gremolata** is great on asparagus, pasta and beans. Simply blitz together the grated zest of 2 lemons, a garlic clove and a handful of flat-leaf parsley.

A North African marinade, **chermoula** works well on grilled vegetables, couscous and freekeh. Blitz a large bunch of fresh coriander leaves, 1 tbsp ground cumin, 2 tbsp olive oil, 4 peeled garlic cloves, 1 tsp paprika, the juice of 1 lemon and sea salt to taste in a food processor until you get a paste.

Sourdough breadcrumbs can be sprinkled on your food to give texture, as well as flavour. Use them in soups and burgers, and on gratins.

Soya

One thing you are likely to start eating more of as a vegan is the humble soya bean. From it you can make milk, tofu, yoghurt, flour and you can of course eat the bean itself.

Tofu is derided by Westerners as being flavourless. It does have a subtle flavour, but its real asset is its texture and the nutrition within: lots of protein and little fat. Texturally, tofu ranges from extra firm, to medium, to silken. Extra firm to medium can be used in stir-fries, whereas silken is good for desserts or soups. Japanese silken tofu is a whole other texture, like delicate cream. I don't freeze tofu, as I don't like the texture — it goes chewy — but some people like that.

Making your own is less difficult than you might think and certainly a cheaper option; see page 33.

Coconut

Coconut is another of those all-purpose foodstuffs like the soya bean. Each element of the coconut tree can be used: the leaves, the husk for coir matting, the young buds, which are hearts of palm, the shell as a receptacle, the flesh as fresh 'meat' or to extract flour, oil, butter, sugar, milk or cream, and lastly the water as a refreshing drink. The water has on occasion been used in drips as a replacement for blood, plus it has oestrogen qualities, so it's good for the menopause. It's magical stuff and forms part of the creation myths of several cultures. If you want to avoid Alzheimer's, eating coconut can help.

How to Open a Fresh Coconut

When you buy a coconut, shake it to make sure there is still water sloshing inside. The coconut will have three 'eyes', one or two of which will be softer. Pierce two of its eyes with a corkscrew or screwdriver and upend the coconut into a glass to collect the water. Then, to crack it open, you can smash it against a concrete floor; with the back of a machete, cleaver or heavy knife, VERY CAREFULLY tap around the 'equator' line that runs around the coconut and it should just split open (this does work — I've tried it); or find a safe area without breakables, place the coconut in a plastic bag and whack it with a hammer (mind your hands).

You can buy frozen coconut flesh from Asian supermarkets, and dried, sweetened or unsweetened, desiccated coconut. When you buy coconut milk in tins, check that it is a good brand without too many thickeners.

Vinegars & Sourness

Introducing acidity into food is another way of augmenting flavour. My favourites are lemon and lime juice, but there is a whole world of vinegars to be discovered. I have dozens: red and white wine, sherry, cider, Chinese black vinegar, fruit vinegars such as raspberry or pineapple or grain vinegars like malt or rice vinegar. Each one is matched to a certain kind of dish or a different cuisine. I also use subtler acidulents such as verjus or orange juice, or souring agents such as pomegranate molasses or the very sour citric acid (available from Asian shops).

Chillies

The Mexicans know that every chilli has a distinct flavour. You want more than just heat; you want fruit, spice, sweetness, smokiness and differing degrees of heat. If it is difficult to get hold of interesting fresh chillies, you should still have access to dried ones, or tinned chillies in the form of pickled or smoked chipotles, or in adobo sauce (really flavoursome). I like to use dried anchos or guajillos, which are mild, and dried chipotles, which are smoked dried jalapeños. The Peruvian yellow chilli aji amarillo is also good and can be bought in the UK as a paste or dried.

Rarer still are genuine Scotch bonnets — mostly they are habaneros. You can tell by smell: proper Scotch bonnets have a fruity smell, whereas habaneros are just heat. I love the Italian pepperoncini: flavoursome and not too hot fresh, they also make great chilli flakes on pizza and pasta when dried.

How to Prepare Dried Chillies

To get the maximum flavour from a dried chilli, first split it open, shake out the seeds and toast it in a dry frying pan until it softens — this happens very quickly, so don't walk away. Now soak the chilli in enough hot water to cover it. Reserve the liquid and scoop out the chillies, then chop them finely. Try adding soaked chipotle flakes to the Vegan Mayonnaise recipe on page 32.

Harissa is a North African chilli sauce, which is lovely with the Tagine on page 117, or on toast!

Pepper

Pepper is not just black and white — there is a whole range of flavours to explore.

Sichuan is a Chinese peppercorn that has a unique taste and makes your mouth tingle. In Japanese cooking, this is called sansho pepper. Use one of these instead of chilli in Asian cooking.

White pepper fell out of fashion to the big black pepper grinder for years, but for paler dishes, I love it.

Green peppercorns are young black peppercorns. I love them pickled or fresh; the latter you can buy in Asian supermarkets.

Pink pepper is not technically pepper but a berry. It has a lovely flavour and contrasting colour to dress dishes.

Long pepper looks as its name suggests and is often used in Indian cookery.

Salt

I'm a big fan of salt — good sea salt, that is, with all the minerals, metals and nutrients, not ordinary table salt. I salt in the cooking to avoid salting at the table. This way I use less salt. There is good scientific data showing that salt does not increase blood pressure except for the 8% of people who have a salt sensitivity.

I use **rock salt** or **sel gris** for cooking, and Maldon sea salt for finishing and for sauces.

Another salt you may not know about is **tempero**, a herby, large-grained salt from Brazil. I use it for my Canary Island-Style Tempero Salt-Baked Mini Potatoes on page 104.

You can make your own flavoured salts or buy them. I've smoked salt and added lemon zest, rose petals and herbs. Nowadays you can buy specialised salts: black Indian, pink Himalayan, rusty orange, green bamboo, red volcanic Hawaiian.

Rosemary Salt

This is great in bread, and on pizzas, baked potatoes and roast potatoes.

Makes 200g

200g good-quality sea salt, such as fleur de sel or Maldon

Several sprigs of rosemary, finely chopped

Mix the salt and rosemary together and store in a clean, dry jar.

You can do this with any herb: just finely chop or process the herb in a food processor, then combine with the salt. Keep the salt in a dry jar in the fridge or in a sealed bag in the freezer.

Seaweed

The fifth taste, umami, in a sense originates from a seaweed called kombu. It's the seaweed that is used to flavour dashi, the Japanese soup stock whence umami derives. Seaweed is high in flavour and minerals such as iodine. If you buy the dried stuff for your pantry, it never goes off.

Nori are the purple/black sheets of seaweed, which can be eaten raw but are better toasted, that you use to wrap sushi. Korean shops sell this in snack packs and I could scoff it by the sheet. Kids like it too. If you buy the sheets for sushi, sometimes it's necessary to re-toast it. Just pass it over a flame or dry-roast it in a pan very quickly — it will shrivel slightly and crisp up.

Wakame is used in miso and has a soft, minerally taste. A small pinch becomes huge. It's used in salads and soup.

Kombu, a type of kelp used to flavour dashi the simple stock in Japanese cuisine, is not eaten, as the texture is very tough — it's just a flavouring. Use a segment 5–10cm big to flavour broth.

Hijaki needs hydrating and cooking. It can be used in stir-fries or in tofu balls.

Carrageen or **Irish moss**, a red seaweed, has thickening qualities that make it a good replacement for gelatine when setting mousses, panna cotta and jellies.

Dulse is a purple seaweed that you can crumble on rice, or use in bread making or in soups. It can also be used as chewing gum!

Sea lettuce, also known as glasswort, is good for baking parchment to cook things 'en papillote'; it can also be fried.

A rather chic ingredient, **samphire** is often served with fish. But in the vegan diet it is good as a salty texture in quinoa salads or steamed and topped with pumpkin seeds.

Sea kale can be steamed and used like asparagus, but it's very pungent and can be hard to get hold of.

Kelp can be used as an alternative to salt.

Flowers

I use quite a few flowers in my cookery and grow them in my garden for culinary use. Also look out for herb flowers, for instance pretty purple chive flowers, as they are like decorative versions of the herb and they taste similar. Do not eat flowers of the nightshade family (potatoes, tomatoes, aubergines, peppers), sweet pea flowers, hydrangeas or foxgloves.

I've used the flowers of various beans, which again taste like the vegetable they come from, and also courgette flowers. Always inspect inside flowers for creepy crawlies and worse. Other pointers: use unsprayed organic flowers. If the stamen is prominent, remove it.

Nasturtiums are peppery, good in salads and the buds can be pickled.

Cornflowers are more of a garnish.

Cowslip petals are honey-like, good for drinks and syrups.

Hibiscus is acidic and bright red in colour.

With **hollyhocks**, eat just the petals.

With perfumed, pungent **roses**, remove the white heel.

Lavender is perfumed and you can add it to sugar.

Pinks petals can be used as a garnish.

Primroses are small, yellow and slightly sweet.

Tulips can be steamed and stuffed, but remove the stamens.

Violets, ideally parma violets, can be crystallised.

Borage has small, purple flowers, ideal in tea or for garnish; remove the green calyx (the small green 'leaves' that surround the flower).

I've used both flower and leaves of **wild geraniums** in salads and pasta.

You can use the scented leaves from **lemon** or **rose pelargonium** plants in baking.

Day lilies – see recipe on page 160.

Elderflowers can be used for drinks and for flavouring, plus they make great fritters.

I sprinkle **marigolds** on top of salads and bread.

Cooking with Leaves

Vine, pandan, geranium (rose and lemon), fig.

Herbs

Fresh herbs add scent as well as flavour to a dish. Sweet leafy herbs include coriander, dill, fennel, mint, basil, chervil and tarragon. These are good for sauces, and adding later in the dish, plus for garnishing. Base-note herbs tend to be woody: bay (I love this; use it in tomato and creamy sauces), rosemary, oregano, marjoram and thyme. These can be used at the beginning of a sauce and are not diminished by long cooking. When dried, some herbs change flavour: mint and oregano, for instance.

Sugar

Used both in sweet and savoury dishes, every sugar has a specific quality and flavour and should be matched to the dish. Bakers tend to prefer cane sugar to beet sugar.

Types include: cane sugar, palm sugar, fructose, coconut sugar, agave nectar, date syrup, mulberry molasses, maple syrup, carob molasses and brown rice syrup. Liquorice is one of the sweetest substances on earth and can be used in various forms, in tea or a candied sugar version can be ground over desserts. I like to candy nuts, fruit and vegetables as a contrasting flavour and texture (see page 24).

Storecupboard Vegan Stuff You Never Knew Existed

Eggs are so useful and have amazing properties: they bind, they stretch, they colour, they glue, they thicken. Traditional sweet baking is fundamentally about using the qualities of eggs. It is tough to replace all of these qualities, but there are some alternatives. Some of them are familiar, but others will be new to you. You can buy '**egg replacers**', which work well in making meringues or 'egg' pasta. **Ground linseed is referred to in certain vegan circles as 'FLAX EGGS': 1 tbsp ground linseeds soaked in 2½ tbsp water has similar binding properties to egg.** The same effect works with **chia seeds** in place of the linseed. **Arrowroot** makes things glossy. **Cornflour** needs to be cooked out or the flavour stays. **Lotus root flour** is good. **Tapioca flour** is very textural, with a nice gloss and is often used in vegan cheese recipes. **Potato flour** is good for gluten-free people, but do not let the liquid boil. **Sago starch** is good for puddings. **Sahlag** is made from orchid roots, with a floral flavour and smell, and is used in Middle Eastern cooking. **Water chestnut flour** gives fried foods a crisp, nutty coating and is used in Asian cooking.

Dark chocolate is ostensibly vegan, but check the packet, as some dark chocolate brands add powdered milk.

Vegan, plant-based alternatives to jelly and gelatine are available but do not have the mouthfeel of jelly, which melts at body temperature. **Carageen or Irish Moss** is derived from seaweed (see page 20). **Agar agar** is used in Asia and sets quite hard, so use sparingly.

Techniques: The Vegan Way

Vegans need to do a great deal of preparation. Arm yourself with the right equipment to make life easier: a sharp vegetable knife, a decent peeler, a julienne peeler, canner, pressure cooker, mandolin and 2 Microplanes (fine and coarse). More expensive but essential is a good, powerful blender such as a Vitamix. Other less essential equipment would be a dehydrator, a stovetop smoker and a spiraliser for making vegetable 'ribbons'.

Sauerkraut

Food fermentation is when food breaks down and converts sugar to either lactic acid or alcohol. It is a bacteria, but a healthy one like penicillin, and aids in the preservation of food. Alcohol, pickles, yoghurt and sourdough are fermented foods. Eating more fermented foods will boost your immune system as it is naturally probiotic. The health benefits of fermentation are known all over the world: the Japanese macrobiotic diet encourages the consumption of pickles because they aid digestion, while in Eastern Europe, cabbage is fermented whole in barrels. You can ferment most foods and salt is the key ingredient that prevents them from rotting. Real sauerkraut takes time — it should be fermented slowly. The proportion of salt is 3 tablespoons for every 2kg of cabbage.

Makes a medium container

1 white cabbage

2 tbsp rock salt

1 tbsp dill seeds

1 tbsp juniper berries

1 apple, cored and thinly sliced or grated

Remove any outer cabbage leaves that may be damaged and chop the cabbage into ribbons. Mix it with the salt, dill seeds, juniper berries and apple in a food-grade plastic container.

Leave it for an hour, then start to 'punch' the cabbage, pummelling it to make it softer. Then place a weight on top of it, such as a glass jar filled with water. Leave overnight, but every so often press down the weight. Eventually the cabbage ribbons should be covered with the saline liquid. If not, cover the cabbage with (ideally bottled) water.

Mix with your hands, pressing down. Cover completely and leave it for a couple of weeks. If then it has a tangy, fermented flavour, put it into sterilised jars (see page 13). If there is any white mould, just scoop that off — it's completely safe. If it hasn't yet fermented, cover it well again and leave for another week or two.

Baechu Kimchi

Kimchi is an ancient Korean sauerkraut. In Korea they have aged kimchis, and they even bury it underground in clay pots over winter so that the frost will break down the cabbage. You can eat your homemade kimchi immediately or after a day, after a week, after a year, but the longer it is left to ferment, the better tasting and the sourer it becomes.

Makes a medium container

200g coarse sea salt

2 litres cold water

2 heads of Chinese leaf (Peking cabbage)

15g garlic, finely chopped

15g ginger, peeled and finely grated (I keep a stick in the freezer and grate it directly with a Microplane)

75g gochugaru Korean red pepper powder (available online)

30g caster sugar

5 spring onions, chopped into 5mm slices

In a food-grade plastic container or other non-reactive container, mix the salt with the water.

Separate the cabbage leaves and place them in the salted water (you could also put the whole heads in). Make sure everything is submerged, then put a plate over the top and a glass jar filled with water on top of that. Soak for 24 hours so that the leaves become soft and pliable, then drain, rinse and squeeze dry.

In the meantime, blend the garlic, ginger, red pepper powder and sugar together in a food processor.

Put the drained cabbage leaves back into the plastic container in layers, spreading the chilli mixture and spring onions between each layer, until all the cabbage is used up.

Pack the seasoned cabbage, rolling up the leaves, into a sterilised glass Kilner or similar jar (see page 13), and let it ferment in a cool place for 3 days before eating.

If you want to try fermenting it for longer, check it every few days to make sure it isn't building up too much gas in the jar (just open the top of the jar a little to check).

Watermelon Rind Pickle

I've pickled walnuts, onions, cucumbers, cherries, lemons, limes, onions and cauliflower. Pickles are good for you, with zero fat, and add zing to your food. This is a Southern-style pickle, beloved of Elvis and Dolly.

Makes 2 x 500ml jars

1 small watermelon

200ml white wine vinegar

100ml water

200g sugar

2 tbsp sea salt

Thumb of ginger, peeled and chopped

1 cinnamon stick, broken in half

2 cloves

Working in segments, peel the green outer skin off the watermelon and remove the reddish pink flesh, scraping off the layer next to the skin with a spoon so that you are left with just the white part. Cut this into 3cm squares or strips.

Put the vinegar, water, sugar, salt, ginger, cinnamon and cloves into a very large saucepan. Bring to the boil, dissolving the sugar, then add the watermelon rind. Bring to the boil again, then simmer for a minute. Remove from the heat and leave it to cool for an hour.

Ladle the watermelon rind into 2 sterilised 500ml jars (see page 13). Cover the rinds with the vinegar mixture, leaving 1cm of headroom at the top. Cover with sterilised lids and keep in the fridge overnight, then it's ready to eat the next day. It will keep for just over a week.

Candied Courgette Strips

Another cooking and preservation method that adds variety to vegan cookery is candying. Rather than adding salt to preserve a vegetable as in pickling, one adds sugar. I like to candy citrus peel, fruits, nuts, vegetables such as beetroot, herbs such as angelica and flowers such as rose petals. These courgette strips can be added to desserts or even salads! Unusual!

Makes a small bowlful

200g caster sugar

175ml water

1 courgette, sliced lengthways using a mandolin

Dissolve the sugar in the water in a medium saucepan over a medium heat. Once dissolved, add the courgette strips and simmer until translucent. Remove from the heat and allow to cool. Lay the strips, spreading them out flat, on a silicone mat or sheet of baking parchment and let them dry in a dehydrator or a very low oven (100°C/gas lowest setting) about an hour until crispy.

Sprouting Alfalfa

'Sprouting' means germinating seeds, which you may have done at school to grow mustard and cress. You can sprout alfalfa, chickpeas, lentils, mung beans, quinoa, peanuts, fenugreek seeds… What do you think bean sprouts are? The sprouts of mung beans! Top chefs love their micro-greens, tiny versions of salads, herbs and vegetables including my favourite, tendrilly delicate pea shoots. Get sprouting seeds, grains and pulses for vibrancy and crunchiness in your diet. You can buy a special sprouting jar or create one yourself with a jam jar, an elastic band and a piece of muslin. Make sure the seeds are not stale and rinse them well before starting.

1–2 tbsp alfalfa seeds

Add enough seeds to cover the bottom of a jam jar in a single layer. Rinse thoroughly, then add 5–10cm water. Cover the jar with a piece of muslin, secure with an elastic band and leave to soak overnight. Drain the water out through the muslin lid. Add another 5–10cm water, shake, strain, cover and leave overnight — and repeat every day for 5–6 days. You will have a lovely jar bursting full of nutritious sprouts.

This is the simplest technique. Other techniques include putting damp cotton wool, then a sheet of folded kitchen paper in the base of an empty plastic vegetable container that has holes to drain. Dampen the cotton wool and spread the seeds on top of the kitchen paper.

If you want to get fancy and start growing chic micro-greens, think about investing in a little perlite (available from garden centres) and cover the bottom of a plastic vegetable container with it, about 1.5cm deep. Set the container in a dish and add a little water to the dish. Cover the perlite with a layer of seeds/beans/nuts and place it somewhere light and warm. The perlite will soak up the water and nourish and hydrate the seeds. You will have usable shoots in 2–4 days. Scissor off the tops to harvest.

Dehydrated Kiwi Fruit

An innovative but actually old-fashioned preserving technique that many chefs, including vegans, are using is dehydration. This is the concept behind powdered vegetable stock or dried soup stock, which is, fundamentally, portable soup, relied upon by sailors and explorers and campers. You will perhaps have used sun-dried tomatoes. Modern chefs scatter dried fruit powders over

desserts, and ingredients like dried beetroot powder are fantastic for colouring pasta and tofu. Dehydration is also the theory behind fruit leather (see page 58). You can buy a dehydrator, use the bottom oven of an Aga or a normal oven with just the light on or on its lowest setting of 60°C. You can also use the sun to dehydrate if you live in a hot country. When dehydrating fruit, choose mature but firm, undamaged fruits. To dehydrate vegetables, do not cook beforehand if it is something you could eat raw; if you would usually cook it, then steam the vegetable for 5–8 minutes before drying.

Kiwi fruit, peeled and very thinly sliced

Place the slices of kiwi in a single layer on a wire rack set over a flat baking tray and dry out overnight or for at least 8 hours in the oven, on its lowest setting, about 60°C. After that, keep checking every couple of hours until the slices are thin but pliable. If you want a powder, continue to dry, then grind in a food processor. Store in a dry, sealed container.

Hot-Smoked Marinated Tofu

I run a monthly supper club called The Secret Garden Club with a gardener colleague called Ms Zia Mays. We've done several smoking workshops to teach people how to smoke. It's seen as quite a macho skill, but it isn't at all. Girls can smoke! We've come a long way baby. There are three main types of smoking: cold, hot and tea smoked. The most complicated is cold smoking, which is how smoked salmon is created. Hot smoking is much quicker than cold; but the easiest method of all is tea smoking, as it can be done on a normal kitchen hob with an old saucepan, a steamer basket and a lid. The tea-smoking mixture comprises loose leaf tea, raw long-grain rice and brown sugar. This hot-smoked recipe comes from Zia and it transforms tofu into a dark brown, savoury-sweet tasty food.

Makes 400g

400g firm tofu, drained and sliced around 4—5mm thick

For the marinade:

3 tbsp soy sauce

3 tbsp maple syrup

3 tbsp olive oil

1 tsp sesame oil

2 tsp Dijon mustard

Mix all the marinade ingredients together in a shallow dish. Slide the tofu slices in, cover and marinate in the fridge for 4 hours or more.

Get the hot smoker ready, then lift the tofu pieces onto a piece of foil on the rack and hot smoke for 30 minutes. Some find the smoky flavour of the tofu quite strong, so you can experiment by smoking for just 15 minutes, say, and then checking whether the flavour is right for you.

Stock

Basic vegetable stock is necessary in particular for soups. If you don't have time to make your own stock, do by all means use a good-quality powdered stock such as Marigold. But from time to time, make the effort to prepare fresh vegetable stock, as it tastes so much more alive than powdered stock.

Vegetable Stock

Excellent stock can be eaten without anything else, as a pure essence of vegetable clear soup. It becomes a broth when other elements are included such as solid vegetables, rice, pasta or beans. You could start a couple of days beforehand with a bowl for scraps of other meals to use in your stock.

Makes about 2 litres

2—3 tbsp olive oil

1—2 large onions, unpeeled, chopped

450g carrots, washed but unpeeled, chopped

450g celery, chopped

3 garlic cloves, peeled

1 bay leaf

10 black peppercorns

2.5 litres water

2 tsp sea salt

50ml soy, tamari or Maggi Liquid Seasoning or Braggs Liquid Aminos, or 1 tbsp Marmite

Any vegetable scraps from other meals (leeks, mushrooms, peppers, turnips, greens, courgettes, fennel, celery leaves. The only rule is: don't use starchy vegetables)

Parsley, including stems

Put the oil, onions, carrots and celery in a large, heavy-bottomed saucepan over a medium heat and sauté them briefly. Then add the garlic, bay, black peppercorns and water. Cook for an hour and then add the salt and soy or other sauce and the parsley. Simmer for another 30 minutes.

Using a chinois (a special conical, fine-meshed sieve) or a sieve lined with a piece of muslin, strain the stock into another large pan or a jug. Squeeze the muslin to get the remaining vegetable juice into the stock (or press the vegetables down in the chinois using the back of a small ladle).

Leave the strained stock to cool, then either freeze or keep in the fridge for up to 3 days. If you want to keep it for longer, boil it up again after a couple of days, adding more vegetables. In the old days, a pot of stock would be kept constantly on the go and, as it reduced, more would be added.

Dashi

This is the vegan version of the Japanese stock that forms the basis of miso soup. Do not boil this stock.

Makes about 1 litre

8cm square of kombu

1 litre water

Put the kombu and water into a pan over a low heat. After approximately 10 minutes, small bubbles will form and the kombu will begin to float.

Remove the kombu and bring the liquid just to the boil, then quickly take the pan off the heat and add ½ cup of cold water, to reduce the temperature.

Strain through a sieve lined with kitchen paper or muslin, and use within 3 days.

How to Cook Vegetables Well

We British have a poor reputation when it comes to cooking vegetables; we boil them to death so that they end up limp, flaccid and devoid of flavour. But I think we have learnt a thing or two over the years. Cut vegetables into even sizes and they will all cook at the same rate.

To blanch, plunge a fruit or vegetable into boiling water for a minute; this will make the skin easier to remove. If you want vegetables to retain their vivid green colour, 'refresh' them in ice-cold water immediately after boiling briefly in salted water. This is known as 'blanch and shock'. Use this technique if you want to cook ahead, or if the vegetable is denser and takes too long to sauté.

To boil, bring a pan of water to the boil on the hob before adding the vegetables. Salting the water will make it boil quicker. Try to have your vegetables in the water for as little time as possible: as soon as they are 'al dente', whip them out. For green vegetables, use a large quantity of water.

To steam means to cook vegetables over boiling water using a steamer or colander and a lid to keep the steam in. This method ensures the vegetables don't become waterlogged. A tagine is a steaming method: the condensation from the water in the vegetables rises up the cone and comes down again to sit in the bottom.

Braising is very useful when cooking delicate vegetables such as asparagus; using little water means that the food does not lose its flavour or become soggy. Use a wide frying pan with a little oil and lightly fry the asparagus, then add a couple of centimetres of boiling, salted water or stock, to finish it off. To stew vegetables means to cook them for a long time in a casserole — useful for root vegetables or potatoes.

Roasting in the oven is one of my favourite methods of cooking. There is less preparation time needed: just clean the vegetables, toss them in oil and herbs in a baking tin and let them roast in the oven on a high heat. Roasting caramelises the vegetables and is particularly effective with root vegetables and of course potatoes.

Sautéeing and frying are normally done over a high heat on a hob, meaning that the vegetables cook quickly. Heat the pan first, then add the oil; once the oil begins to shimmer, add the vegetables. The oil should not be smoking. If it is, remove it carefully from the heat until it stops smoking and cools down. For sautéeing, fry vegetables in a shallow frying pan, moving and turning with tongs or a fish slice to stop them burning. You can also deep-fry; in which case, the fat you use should generally be at 180—190°C and make sure you submerge the vegetables in the oil. Deep-frying at the correct heat shouldn't result in greasy vegetables; in fact, the heat seals the outside, preventing the oil from entering the vegetable. This is fabulous for tempura style vegetables: add a light batter and deep-fry. With both frying and sautéeing, do not overcrowd the pan.

Stir-frying is the Asian version of sautéeing, authentically done at such a high heat that you need a water tap to cool down the outside of the wok. Ingredients should be already prepped, cooked quickly in order of length of cooking, so tougher vegetables go in first.

Grilling and barbecuing cause vegetables to cook on the outside first, giving a smoky, blackened, charcoal flavour. Brush oil on the outside, along with minced garlic and herbs, and grill mushrooms, peppers, tomatoes, courgettes and aubergines.

Substitutes: Vegan DIY

You've got two choices when it comes to vegan foods: try to imitate the carnivore diet with substitutes, or develop an entirely different way of eating, less dependent on straight-up protein. Still, most vegans have been raised on a 'normal' diet and from time to time crave the comforting foods they know and recognise. The following section explains the alternatives and substitutes. Some are easier than others.

Nut Milk & Cream

You will need a high-speed blender and a muslin bag or gauze to make your own nut (or seed) milk and cream. You can buy inexpensive nut milk bags on Amazon or use a jelly strainer. In the fridge, the milk should last 3—5 days. Use in cereal or drinks, or any cooking. The cashew cream can be frozen. It's the same technique for both milk and cream — the difference is simply in the quantity of water used.

For milk (1 litre):

200g almonds, cashew nuts, hazelnuts, macadamia nuts, unsweetened coconut flakes, hemp seeds, pumpkin seeds or sunflower seeds

900ml water (preferably filtered or bottled to keep the taste as neutral as possible)

For sweet milk: 2—4 stoned dates, 1 tbsp agave nectar, 1 tsp vanilla paste or ¼ tsp ground cinnamon

For cream:

300g cashew nuts

150—300ml water, depending on how thick you want the cream

Pinch of sea salt (for savoury) or 4 dates, stoned, and ½ tsp vanilla paste (for sweet)

Soak the nuts in the water for at least 2 hours but preferably overnight. Drain the nuts and place with the water and either the savoury or sweet flavouring, if using, in a powerful blender, such as a Vitamix. Whizz on high speed for about 1 minute, then strain through a muslin bag or a chinois into a jug or bottle. If it separates, just stir or shake. See Cashew Nut, Banana & Apricot Smoothie on page 62.

Coconut Whipped Cream

Serves 4–6

2 x 400ml tins of coconut milk

150g caster sugar

1 tsp vanilla paste

You want just the creamy part of the coconut milk, so turn the tin over, open it and scoop off the hard cream, leaving the water. In a stand mixer or using an electric whisk, mix the sugar and vanilla paste into the cream. Use to top any dessert, or as a side with pudding.

Thick Soya Cream

Serves 2–4

40ml sweetened soya milk

1 tsp vanilla paste

2 tbsp agave nectar, or brown rice or maple syrup

160ml neutral oil (I prefer to use sweet cold-pressed almond oil)

Pour the soya milk into a blender, add the vanilla and syrup, then, with the motor running, slowly pour in the oil.

This can also be piped.

Soya Yoghurt

Of course, you can buy soya yoghurt in most places now, but if you want to try making your own, here is a recipe. You will need to buy a starter soya yoghurt, however.

Makes 1 litre

1 litre soya milk (sweetened or unsweetened)

Pinch of sea salt

10g agar agar or 2 tbsp ground linseed

125g pot of good-quality plain soya yoghurt

Flavourings, if desired (fruit/berries/cinnamon)

Shake the soya milk carton and pour it into a medium saucepan. Heat over a medium heat until lukewarm, then let it cool to between 40 and 50°C. Whisk in the salt and agar agar or ground linseed, to thicken.

Then add the soya yoghurt, stir it in and leave it either in a covered pan in a warm place — an airing cupboard or a low oven — or in a yoghurt maker for 6–8 hours or overnight. Then place it in the fridge where it will thicken further. Stir in any flavourings, if desired.

After each batch, keep back 100ml of the old (unflavoured) yoghurt in the fridge to start your next batch.

Vegan Spread

In terms of finding a butter substitute for baking, the commercial soya, sunflower or, even better, homemade vegan spread here are good choices. Coconut oil can also be used on toast. This spread requires ordering a special ingredient over the internet: liquid soy lecithin. It's relatively cheap and will last a long time, as you don't use much in the recipe. The other unusual ingredient is xanthan gum, which can often be found in the baking sections of supermarkets. People on a gluten-free diet use it for baking, as it adds stretchiness. Once you have these two ingredients, this recipe is easy, and it tastes really good. Being made of coconut oil, it's also very good for you and not too processed. Instead of adding salt, you can add another flavouring of your choice, such as Marmite or nutritional yeast, or you can add finely chopped garlic with the salt.

Makes 250g

1 tsp cider vinegar

160ml unsweetened soy milk

160g organic coconut oil

1 tsp rapeseed oil

1 tsp liquid soy lecithin

¼ tsp xanthan gum

1 tsp Maldon sea salt

Add the cider vinegar to the soya milk and let it curdle for about 30 seconds. Melt the coconut oil until just liquid but not hot, in 15-second bursts in a microwave or in a saucepan on the hob. It's important not to let it get too hot.

Put the melted coconut oil and rapeseed oil in a food processor. Process for a few seconds to make sure it is smooth, then pour in the curdled soya milk, the liquid lecithin and the xanthan gum. Process for a minute until it is a smooth, yellow grease. Add the sea salt and mix well, then scrape using a rubber spatula into a small bowl or a small rectangular (butter-shaped and sized) plastic container. Keep in the fridge for up to about 3 weeks. Great on toast.

Basic Nut Butter

Nut butters are easy to make if you have a good food processor. Just place your chosen seeds or nuts inside and process at a high speed.

Suggestions

Seeds: pumpkin, sunflower, sesame (for tahini), linseed or a mix.

Nuts: almonds, cashew, macadamia, brazil, pistachio, pecan, walnuts, peanuts (see overleaf), unsweetened coconut flakes.

Flavourings: fruit, maple syrup, cinnamon, salt, vanilla or chocolate for 'Nutella'. You could also sweeten butters with fruit, as in almond and apple butter or maple syrup, or with a spice, as in walnut and cinnamon butter.

If the seeds or nuts are lightly roasted beforehand, they are easier to blend into a creamy paste. If using raw, you may need to add some good-quality oil to get spreadability (coconut, walnut or flax oil, for instance). If using a blender or Vitamix, you will also need to add oil.

Peanut Butter

Makes a 200g jar

200g nuts, raw or ready-roasted

2 tbsp cold-pressed oil

½—1 tsp sea salt

If you want to roast raw nuts (which brings out the oils), preheat your oven to 180°C/gas mark 4. Spread the nuts in a single layer on a baking tray and bake for 10 minutes or until lightly golden. Then continue with the rest of the recipe while the nuts are still warm.

To make both raw and roasted nut butter, put the nuts in a high-speed blender or food processor. Pulse a couple of times in 30-second intervals, scraping down between pulses. Then add the oil and salt. Pulse again until smooth, unless you want chunky peanut butter. You can store this in a jar or plastic container in the fridge for at least a month.

Vegan Mayonnaise

This basic 'vegannaise' recipe can be flavoured any which way: suggestions below. I've had non-vegan friends try this, and they prefer it to real mayonnaise. It's good on avocado, in salad, on everything.

Makes a 500ml jar

250ml soya milk

250ml olive or rapeseed oil

2 tbsp cider vinegar

A squeeze of lemon juice

Sea salt

Put the soya milk in a blender and, with the motor running, add the oil very slowly in a stream. Then add the vinegar and lemon juice and you'll see the mixture coagulate instantly. Season with salt and add a flavouring, if you like (see below). Put in a jar and refrigerate.

You could also treat this as a vegan Provençal aïoli by adding a couple of cloves of finely chopped garlic and using it as a sauce with lightly cooked florets of cauliflower, green beans, green olives and *potatoes à la vapeur* (boiled) with salt and a bay leaf.

Suggested flavourings: mustard, chipotle chillies, garlic.

Basic Nut 'Cheez'

If you've had real dairy cheese any time recently, you're going to find it hard to forget what it tastes like. And in that frame of mind, any non-dairy substitute is going to be rather disappointing. On this basis, I must admit I was cynical about this, but it was delicious and I couldn't stop eating it. It's equivalent to a soft goats' cheese or cream cheese.

Makes about 300g

100g macadamia nuts

100g cashew nuts

About 1 tsp sea salt

Flavouring, such as herbs, spices or chilli

Soak all the nuts overnight, then drain off the excess water. Blend in a powerful blender, adding salt and any flavouring. Then transfer the mixture to a muslin-lined sieve set over a bowl, or a nut bag. Wrap the mixture with the muslin, press it down and leave weighted with a jar filled with water for 24 hours. Then serve! Great on crackers.

Smoky Chipotle Cashew Cheese

This is a firmer-textured cheese, a bit like a Gouda perhaps, and with a deep, smoky flavour.

Makes 6 small cheeses

300g raw (unroasted) cashew nuts

6 sun-dried tomatoes, snipped into small pieces (optional)

Vegetable or olive oil spray

50g nutritional yeast

80g organic coconut oil

1 tbsp white miso

1 tbsp cider vinegar

1 tsp sea salt

1 tsp mustard powder

½ tsp smoked paprika

2 tbsp liquid smoke

1 tbsp chipotle paste

Soak the cashews in cold water overnight, with the sun-dried tomato pieces, if using, then drain. Spray 6 ramekins with oil.

In a blender, pulse the drained cashews and sun-dried tomatoes, if using, with all the remaining ingredients. You can add a couple of tablespoons of warm water to the blender if you feel the mixture is too stiff.

Using a rubber spatula, scrape the 'cheese' mixture into the prepared ramekins. Store in the fridge. Upend the ramekins, flipping out the cheeses, when you want to use them.

Block Tofu & Soya Milk

You will need to buy a coagulant. I recommend 'nigari' crystals, which can be bought online. You can also use sodium chloride, Epsom salts or lemon juice, but in my tests nigari was the best. I also invested in a plastic tofu mould, although you can use ordinary kitchenware, for instance a plastic Tupperware-style box with holes punched in the bottom, to achieve a similar effect. You will also need a muslin and a metal sieve.

Makes an 800g block of tofu

500g dried soya beans

2½ tbsp nigari (I used crystals)

Firstly, soak the soya beans overnight (for at least 8 hours) in a large bowl, covered with cold tap water. They start out as little round pellets, but as they expand, they become bean shaped.

Put 2.5 litres fresh water into the largest saucepan you have and place over a medium heat to start warming.

Meanwhile, drain the beans and grind with 1 litre fresh water in a powerful blender or Vitamix. You'll probably have to do this in 2 batches. Add the finely ground bean mixture to the pan and heat until it reaches a temperature of around 70°C.

Then take a cup of the water-bean mixture from the pan and add it to the blender to rinse out the rest of the beans. Pour this into the pan and heat for around 10 minutes, taking care not to scorch the bottom of the pan.

Put a piece of muslin into a metal sieve set over a bowl. Pour enough of the bean mixture to fill the sieve and press down. When you have squeezed most of the soya milk out of the mixture, you will be left with the soya bean lees, also known as okara, which can be used in baking or to make burgers.

Empty the muslin of okara into a clean bowl. Keep straining, squeezing and setting aside the okara until all the contents of your large saucepan have been emptied. You will now have soya milk in your bowl (and may need to use an extra bowl or jug to contain it), which you can use for your tofu, or remove some for use in tea, coffee or smoothies. You can stop at this stage if all you want is soya milk.

Now take the okara in batches, place it back in the muslin, tie the top together and squeeze a second pressing of milk out of the beans. This pressing is important because it gets the last remnants of thick milk from the beans. You'll need another bowl at this point, to put the exhausted beans in. Continue until you have pressed all of the okara a second time.

Now put all of the soya milk, first and second pressing, back into the large saucepan. Heat gently until it reaches 70–80°C, no hotter. This is the point where you can add flavouring, such as citrus zest, yuzu paste or sesame seeds, beetroot powder or finely chopped herbs such as basil or coriander, or herb oil, if you so choose.

Once it has reached the temperature required, take it off the heat and add the nigari, which will coagulate the mixture. You don't want to add too much because the coagulants can make the tofu taste bitter, although once your tofu is formed, you can gently rinse it to get rid of any lingering bitterness.

Put a lid on the pan and wait 10 minutes, after which the soya milk will have separated into curds and whey, just as if you were making dairy cheese.

Rinse out the muslin and place it in the tofu mould (see introduction). Using a slotted ladle, carefully scoop out some curds and place them in the lined mould. Continue with the remaining curds. You can discard the whey but there are uses for it — you could give it to plants! Cover the top of the tofu with the muslin.

Finally, you need to press the tofu to get a compact block. If you have a dedicated tofu mould, you can put it in the press that comes with it and weight it down with cans of food. Otherwise, use a Tupperware container or a colander and place a small plate and some cans on top to weight it down.

After half an hour, gently rinse the tofu in cold water, by pouring a few cups of water on it rather than running the tap directly on the tofu, especially if it is very delicate, or it will break up. Keep the rinsed tofu in a container of cold water in the fridge. It will keep for up to 7 days, but do change the water every day or so.

The Colour Wheel of Food

Part of the balanced diet is thinking not just in terms of flavour but of colour, both contrasting and complementary. 'Eat your greens' is not just a phrase meted out by concerned parents; it's based on fact: green food, particularly dark green leafy vegetables, is good for you. In Chinese medicine, there are links between the organs, taste and colour.

Consumers buy food based on their colour: it is no coincidence that supermarkets use pink light on meat to make it look healthier and brighter. When eating, try to develop what some people call 'rainbow' eating, i.e. working your way through a variety of colours during the course of the day to ensure you are eating a varied mix of nutrients.

We are acutely sensitive to the colour of our food, so this is a little exploration of the colour wheel from a health and vitamin point of view.

Black

There are no truly black foods, except for grapes and olives perhaps; most 'black' foods tend to be dark purple.

Purple, violet or mauve is a royal colour, a biblical hue, a rare and expensive dye prior to synthetic dyes. Sumptuary laws prevented commoners from wearing it. Lately it has become associated with women's suffrage and feminism. Dark foods contain anthocyanins, good for eye health, anti-ageing and protecting against cancer and high blood pressure.

Blackberries, sprouting broccoli, Peruvian potatoes, plums, blueberries, aubergines, purple sprouting broccoli, grapes, lavender, beetroot, purple yams, figs, grapes, red cabbage.

Brown

Brown is the colour of the earth, often grown under the ground. Brown signifies natural, unbleached, unprocessed, real, rustic. I've included legumes here because they are dried vegetables.

Roots, turnips, swede, potatoes, mushrooms, pulses, nuts, wheat, lentils, chickpeas, mung beans, onions, yams.

Green

Greens used to be the colour of sex rather than red but symbolises growth, renewal, youth, fertility, money, land, nature, spring. Mary Magdalene wears green in art, while the Virgin Mary wears blue, the colour of heaven. Green is now associated with conservation and ecology, morality. You could say this colour has had all the fun drained out of it. What a shame.

Good for the liver and detoxing; anti Alzheimer's; the darker the better. Contains chlorophyll, apigenin, luteolin and isothiocyanates.

Dark Green

Kale, cavolo nero, broccoli, spinach, watercress.

Medium Green

Artichokes, green lentils, mangetout, limes, runner beans, bok choi, lamb's lettuce, rocket, chives, spring onions, kiwi fruit, apples, limes, gooseberries, grapes, green tea, wasabi, capers.

Light Green

Lettuce, peas, Brussels sprouts, cabbage, Chinese cabbage, greengages, cristophenes, leeks, courgettes, endives, tomatillos, herbs, avocados, cucumber, mangetout, celery, cress, asparagus.

Red

Red signifies ripeness, heat, energy, the ability to fight. Anti-cancer properties, cardiovascular conditions, contains resveratrol, an element of the 'French Paradox' (in which French people who drink red wine have lower incidences of heart disease), lycopene (anti-prostate cancer) and capsaican, which gives you a natural high.

Peppers, tomatoes, chillies, beetroot, red cabbage, strawberries, apples, watermelons, radishes, rhubarb, raspberries, red onions, pomegranates, cranberries, cherries, red wine.

Orange to Yellow

Orange signifies sunshine, optimism, summer, gold.

Contains carotenoids, good for skin health and elasticity, healthy bones and stomach. Many fruits are in the yellow to red spectrum including vegetables that are botanically fruit such as tomatoes, peppers and pumpkins. Citrus contains limonoids, anti-cancer agent, so grate lemon zest onto everything.

Sweet potatoes, carrots (containing alpha carotene, which the body processes into vitamin A), corn (lutein and zeaxanthin benefit eyesight), pumpkins/squash and squash blossoms, turmeric root (contains curcumin, an antioxidant and anti-fat), persimmons, oranges, mandarins, tangerines, clementines, kumquats (contain beta-cryptoxanthin, good for eyesight and healthy bones), pineapple and papaya (contain bromelain, an anti-inflammatory), grapefruit, lemons, melon, mangoes, apricots, peaches, nectarines, parsnips, bananas, melon, swedes, passionfruit, cape gooseberry or physalis, jackfruit, quince.

White

White is associated with wealth, purity and being rich enough not to work outdoors. Rich people ate white bread and white sugar in the past, and the poor tried to emulate them. Now rich people eat brown bread! White food is often bleached and therefore has fewer vitamins. Good for the immune system, and possesses diuretic properties.

Butter beans, cauliflower, celeriac, asparagus, mushrooms, potatoes, soya beans, garlic, daikon radishes, parsnips, salsify, coconuts.

Forced rhubarb and forced chicory are paler than their 'unforced' versions. The lack of light means they are ivory coloured and tender.

The missing colour is blue. One of the few true blue foods is blue corn. Hence in professional kitchens the plasters (and kitchen roll) are blue, because you can easily pick them out if they drop in the food.

Snacks

Vegans, like everybody else, get hungry when they are on the move, but vegan fast food is not always readily available. Naturally there is the old standby: fruit and nuts. We all love to snack between meals, and while the French may say this is not a good thing, it's especially important for vegans to have a few energy boosters to stave off low blood sugar. This is probably one of the most important chapters of this book. Having a few snacks that you know how to make quickly and easily, as opposed to lengthier meals with lots of prep, is essential. Some of these can be made in advance for lunchboxes and pick-me-ups.

13 Things on Toast

Of course, I'm a Marmite lover, which is vegan, and I grew up with Marmite on toast for breakfast. My whole family are toast fiends. Toast is more than breakfast — it's an all-day thing. It's an all-night thing too. If I can't sleep, I get up and make toast. Yes, I have crumbs in my bed.

For each 'recipe' below, spread the contents on in the given order, starting with good bread, toasted or otherwise, or oatcakes, or rice cakes or whatever! Each 'recipe' serves one and will top 2 slices of toast, or bread in the case of Number 3.

1 Strawberries, balsamic vinegar, black pepper

Coconut oil or vegan cream cheese

4–5 strawberries, sliced

Balsamic vinegar, for drizzling

Black pepper

2 White miso, radishes, dill

2 tbsp white miso

4–5 radishes, thinly sliced

A few fronds of dill

3 Olive oil, brown sugar

2 slices of bread

Big slug of good olive oil

3 tbsp brown sugar

4 Cinnamon toast

Grill one side of the bread, then add the toppings and grill the other side to caramelise the sugar.

Coconut oil or vegan spread

1–2 tbsp ground cinnamon

1–2 tbsp brown sugar

5 Dark chocolate spread, hazelnuts

4 tbsp vegan dark chocolate spread

Scattering of chopped toasted hazelnuts

A little sea salt

6 Black or green tapenade

(This is also a good canapé)

4 tbsp black or green tapenade

½ lemon, thinly sliced

7 The healthy Elvis

Peanut butter

1 banana, sliced or mashed

Drizzle of maple syrup

8 Marmite, tahini, alfalfa sprouts

Coconut oil or vegan spread

Marmite

Tahini

Alfalfa sprouts

9 Peanut butter, red chilli jam

3 tbsp crunchy peanut butter

2 tbsp red chilli jam

10 Avocado, chilli

1 ripe avocado

Squeeze of lime juice

Scattering of dried chilli flakes

11 Tomatoes, garlic, olive oil

1 garlic clove, to rub on the toast

2 medium tomatoes, thinly sliced

Olive oil, for drizzling

Sea salt and freshly ground pepper

Small handful of basil leaves, to garnish

12 Tahini, maple or date syrup

Similar principle to the olive oil/brown sugar combo: the fudgy nuttiness of tahini is a lovely counterpoint to either maple or date syrup.

2 tbsp tahini

2 tbsp maple or date syrup

13 Spicy cashew cheese

4 tbsp Smoky Chipotle Cashew Cheese (see page 33)

A few slices of fresh red chilli (optional)

42

Sushi Rice

Although Japanese food is known for its fresh fish, it's easy to make vegan sushi. Sushi and onigiri (below) are treated as snack food in Japan. I think they are the perfect plane food. (If you are travelling, another option is to order the Asian meal, which is usually vegan and pretty good.)

It is fiddly making sushi, but keep practising. I had a Japanese cookery lesson with Hiromi Stone and she emphasised the importance of fresh 'new season' rice, so check the dates on the packet! She prefers Californian sushi rice rather than Italian, as it is better quality. Authentic Japanese sushi rice is quite expensive.

300g sushi rice

360ml water

1 tsp sea salt

80ml rice vinegar

Rinse the rice in a sieve. Repeat at least 3 times until the water runs clear. Put the rice and water in a medium saucepan, cover and place over a high heat until the water boils, then turn it down to a simmer and add the salt. Cook, covered, for 15–20 minutes, then remove from the heat and allow to steam for 10–15 minutes, still covered.

Transfer the rice to a shallow, wide bowl and 'fold' it using a wooden spoon or spatula; you are trying to cool down the rice (the Japanese use a fan) and stirring will give it a shine. Add the vinegar and continue to fold the rice until it is cool enough to handle. Do not refrigerate the rice before using in the Onigiri Rice Triangles, as it will go hard.

Onigiri Rice Triangles

Warm cooked sushi rice
  (see above)

Small squares or strips
  of nori seaweed

Sea salt

Suggested fillings:

Umeboshi plums, stoned,
  or umeboshi paste

Shredded carrot or cucumber,
  mixed with a little soy
  sauce

Japanese pickles, such as
  ginger or daikon radish

Have a bowl of warm water nearby when you're assembling these to prevent the rice sticking to your hands.

Wet your hands and put a little salt in the palm of your left hand. Grasp about ½ cup of rice and place it in the palm of the same hand. Make a small well in the centre, place your chosen filling in the well and cover with more rice. Gently but firmly shape into a pyramid, turning as you shape. Wrap with the nori, adding a dab of the filling to the outside for identification purposes. Wrap in clingfilm, if eating on the run!

Crispy Cavolo Nero or Kale Chips

Serves 1 person
(with self-restraint)

Approx. 3—4 large leaves
of cavolo nero or
kale per baking tray,
washed and dried

Generous glug of olive
or nut oil, such as
walnut or avocado

Option 1:

1 heaped tbsp almond
butter

1 tbsp sea salt

Sprinkling of dulse
(purple seaweed) and/
or bright green sea
lettuce

Option 2:

1 tbsp nutritional
yeast

1 tsp sea salt

I don't even like kale, but these are very moreish.
Turns out that Gwyneth Paltrow knows what she is
talking about. Two versions here. I used cavolo nero
which is similar, as I have plenty of it growing in
the garden. It is a fantastic way of making kids eat
greens too. I would do at least 3 baking trays of
these at a time as you get through them very quickly.
(Photo on page 40.)

Preheat the oven to 180°C/gas mark 4. Strip the
leaves either side of the bitter stalk and then
tear again into roughly 3cm-square sections.
Lay them on foil or baking parchment in a single
layer on baking trays.

Option 1: Mix the oil, almond butter and salt
together in a small bowl, then rub the mixture
into the leaves. Bake for about 10 minutes until
crispy, then top with the purple dulse or green
sea lettuce.

Option 2: Mix the oil, nutritional yeast and
salt together, then rub the mixture thoroughly
into the leaves, making sure every bit is
covered. Bake for about 10 minutes until crispy.

Vegan Malt Loaf

Makes 1 large loaf

3 tbsp malt extract
(available online and
in chemists)

100ml golden syrup

100ml date syrup

130ml soya milk

130g (about 18) dates,
stoned

225g self-raising flour

Pinch of sea salt

This is a really fudgy, squidgy, rich recipe that
works well with the Roasted Carrot Dip on page 52.
Malt extract contains lots of iron and vitamins.
(Photo on page 48.)

Preheat the oven to 190°C/gas mark 5. Grease and
line a large (900g/2lb) loaf tin.

Warm the malt extract, golden syrup, date syrup
and soya milk together in a large saucepan, then
fold in the dates, flour and salt.

Tip the mixture into the prepared loaf tin and
bake for 40 minutes.

Nine Dips, and the Rise of Hummus

If you are a vegetarian or vegan, you are bound to have a hummus recipe already. Over the last decade, hummus has become the go-to health food; its share of the market is booming. I remember when UK supermarkets first started selling hummus. It was beige, quite textural and not that nice. It used to be hippie food, earnest stuff that you bought in 70s vegetarian restaurants like Cranks. It was also the brown puddle next to the pink puddle in Greek restaurants.

Since then, it has improved, to the point that the average British supermarket sells tons of it. There are shelves dedicated to hummus: plain, organic, lemon and coriander, jalapeño, red pepper, avocado. Is there anything that hummus doesn't go with? (Actually there is; I once had a posh meal at a London hotel where they served fish on a bed of hot hummus. Truly horrible.)

This dip has become the healthy food for kids' lunchboxes, the standby snack for tired chefs, a vegan staple and loved by Arabs, Israelis, activists and prime ministers.

How many times a day can you eat hummus? In Israel, approximately four times a day and definitely with every meal. 'Hummus' means 'chickpea' in Arabic.

While hummus is so ancient that it is mentioned in the Bible, there is controversy over its cultural appropriation, for Israelis are accused of marketing it as an Israeli product (along with falafel). But let's face it, almost every recipe on the planet is nicked. The story of recipes throughout the world and throughout history boils down to: I like the taste of that, show me how to make it. Then the 'thief' gives the dish some tweaks.

On a visit to Israel, I visited the Strauss factory where they make Sabras hummus, the most popular brand in the United States. "It's all about the garnish," said Ofra Strauss, the president. "In the UK you don't really 'do' garnishes. Also, your hummus is not cooked; it's quite rough. In the States they prefer smooth cooked hummus, which is pasteurised, and they like to have garnishes. Artichokes are one of the most popular toppings." They eat hummus in every part of the US, but the highest concentration is in Boston, where it is scoffed in industrial quantities by students.

One of the food developers at the Strauss factory, when I asked about the differences between Israeli hummus and that of their Arab neighbours, said that hummus in Israel (and Lebanon) has a higher percentage of tahini (25%), less lemon, less spice and less seasoning. This is a general rule with food, he said — there is less spice and seasoning when the country of origin is wealthy, while food is spicier and more flavoured in poorer, more southern countries, with a higher PH (acidity/lemon). Personally, I prefer less tahini and more spice. I'm a peasant when it comes to food.

There are 101 things you can do with hummus, but you can also make dips from other pulses: broad beans, ful medames, lentils... Or in any of the ways on the following pages. Everyone loves dips — they're grown-up baby food.

1 My Basic Hummus

Serves 4–6

125g dried chickpeas and
½ tbsp bicarbonate of
soda, plus a pinch;
or 400g tin/jar of
chickpeas from India

2 tbsp tahini

Juice of ½ lemon

1 tbsp ground cumin

1 tsp ground coriander

Generous glug of good
olive oil

1 garlic clove

Good sea salt

To garnish:

Chickpeas and/or toasted
pine nuts

Paprika

Chopped parsley

If using dried chickpeas, soak them overnight in plenty of cold water with the bicarbonate of soda, then drain and rinse. Place in a large pan, cover with water and add a pinch of salt and another pinch of bicarbonate of soda (not too much, as you want the softening qualities without the soapy flavour). Cook for 2 hours or until soft, topping up the water if necessary to keep them covered. (If you live in an area with soft water, the cooking time may be less. It also depends on the freshness — yes, even of dried chickpeas — and the type of chickpeas.) Once soft, drain and leave to cool.

Whizz the cooked or drained tinned chickpeas, the tahini, lemon juice, cumin, coriander and olive oil together in a food processor or blender. Crush the garlic with at least 1 tbsp salt and add. Taste. You may need more lemon juice. Muck about with seasonings. Top with the garnishes and eat with warm flat bread, such as pitta.

2 Ful Medames Dip

Serves 4–6

100g dried fava (broad)
beans or 400g tin of
ful medames

2 tbsp tahini

2 tbsp olive oil, plus
extra to garnish

Juice of 1 lemon

1 garlic clove, crushed

1 tsp smoked paprika

Sea salt, to taste

Handful of parsley,
chopped, to garnish

'Ful' are dried fava (broad) beans, a pulse made infamous by Hannibal the Cannibal. You can make this Egyptian dip with fresh or frozen broad beans too. Think of it as a funkier, sludgier hummus.

If using dried beans, boil them in water for 30–40 minutes (no need to pre-soak), then drain. Otherwise, drain the tin. Add the beans, tahini, oil, lemon juice, garlic, paprika and some salt to a food processor. Whizz to combine (or mash everything by hand), then tip into a bowl, drizzle over more olive oil and sprinkle with parsley.

(3) Skordalia

Serves 4–6

500g Cypriot
potatoes, peeled
and diced

2–3 garlic cloves,
crushed

50–100ml olive oil

Juice of 1 lemon

Sea salt

For the garnish:

Handful of mint,
finely chopped

Handful of flat-leaf
parsley, finely
chopped

Handful of walnuts,
finely chopped
(optional)

Olive oil, lemon
juice and sea salt

Cypriot potatoes — waxy, red-skinned, firm-fleshed, the Peter Andre of the spud world — are one of the best to make skordalia. Classically Cypriot, this dip sounds rather unglamorous on the page, consisting of cold mashed potatoes, but it's actually very moreish. This is easier if you have a food processor, as it's got to be as silky as a baby's bottom; lumps would ruin it. In the absence of Cypriot potatoes, use any waxy ones.

Put the potatoes into a pan of salted cold water and bring to the boil. Boil for 10 minutes, then drain. Put the garlic, half the potatoes and half the olive oil in a food processor and process until smooth.

Dissolve 1 tbsp salt, or to taste, in the lemon juice, in a jug. Mix the rest of the olive oil into the juice, whisking thoroughly. Add this liquid and the rest of the cooked potatoes to the food processor and process until smooth. Check for seasoning and leave to cool.

For the garnish, mix the herbs and walnuts, if using, with olive oil, lemon juice and salt to taste. Top the skordalia with the garnish and eat with bread, pitta, batons of raw veg, or fried strips of courgette, red pepper and aubergine.

(4) Yellow Pepper Dip with Walnuts

Serves 4–6

2 yellow peppers, roasted, skinned
and deseeded (see opposite)

Handful of walnuts, plus extra,
chopped, to garnish

Juice of 1 lemon or lime

2 garlic cloves, very finely chopped

1–2 tbsp good sunflower or pumpkin seed oil,
plus extra to garnish

Tiny pinch of saffron strands

1 tbsp Maldon sea salt

Blend the roasted peppers, walnuts, juice, garlic and oil in a food processor. Grind the saffron and sea salt with a pestle and mortar. Combine with the blended ingredients in a bowl and garnish with the walnuts and a drizzle of oil.

50

⑤ Red Pepper Dip with Sesame Crostini

Serves 4–6

4 red peppers

1 red chilli

1–2 tbsp good olive oil,
   plus extra for roasting

Juice of 1 lemon

2 garlic cloves, very
   finely chopped

½ tsp ground cumin

½ tsp ground coriander

1 tbsp Maldon sea salt

Nibbed pistachio nuts,
   to garnish (optional)

For the crostini:

½ baguette or ciabatta, thinly
   sliced into rounds

Olive oil, for drizzling

Sea salt, for sprinkling

3 tbsp sesame seeds (white
   or black)

This is a bit like muhammara but even simpler. It takes minutes. I've only put one chilli in, which gives you residual heat without blowing your head off. Deseed the chilli if you don't want too much heat.

Preheat the oven to 200°C/gas mark 6. Roast the peppers and chilli in an oiled baking tray for 20 minutes for the peppers, and 10 minutes for the chilli.

Strip the skin off the peppers and chilli while they are still hot and steamy — much quicker and easier. Discard the seeds and the stems. Whizz the flesh in a blender with the rest of the ingredients except the pistachios. Remove to a bowl and leave to cool.

For the crostini, preheat the oven to 200°C/gas mark 6 (or keep it hot after roasting the peppers and chilli). Grease a baking tray with olive oil and place the bread rounds on the tray. Drizzle the tops with olive oil and scatter with salt and the sesame seeds. Bake for 5 minutes or until lightly golden, then flip and bake for another 2 minutes.

⑥ Guacamole

Serves 2–4

2 ripe Hass avocados

1 jalapeño chilli, roasted,
   skinned and deseeded (see
   recipe above for roasting),
   then finely chopped

1 small red onion, finely diced

Juice of 1 lime

½ tsp ground cumin

Handful of coriander,
   finely chopped

Sea salt, such as fleur de sel
   or Maldon

I make this very simply, the way Mexicans do. No garlic. NO GARLIC. Got it?

Peel, halve and stone the avocados. Chop into cubes, then roughly mash with a fork to make a chunky paste. Don't use a blender or food processor; you want it slightly rough, not whipped like a shop-bought guacamole. Stir in the chilli, onion, lime juice, cumin, 1 tbsp salt and the coriander. Taste and season with salt.

(7) Roasted Carrot Dip

Serves 4–6

6 large, crunchy, sweet carrots, topped, tailed and peeled

2–3 garlic cloves, unpeeled

3 tbsp olive oil, plus extra for roasting

2 tbsp agave nectar

1 tbsp coriander seeds

Juice of ½ lemon

Sea salt

For the garnish:

Organic cold-pressed pumpkin seed oil (the dark petrol-green Styrian oil from Austria is excellent)

Pomegranate or date syrup, or coriander leaves

This makes a good lunch option with the Vegan Malt Loaf (see page 45).

Preheat your oven to 200°C/gas mark 6 and toss the carrots and garlic cloves (in their skins) in some olive oil. Spread out in a roasting tin and roast for 15–20 minutes, then remove from the oven, slip the garlic cloves from their skins and leave to cool.

Put the carrots, garlic, olive oil, agave nectar, coriander seeds, lemon juice and salt to taste in a powerful blender or Vitamix and process until smooth (you can leave it as a rougher texture if you prefer). Drizzle and/or sprinkle over the garnish ingredients to serve.

(8) Soya Tzatziki Dip

Serves 4–6

Maldon sea salt or other good flaky sea salt

1 cucumber, peeled (deseeded if it's not good quality) and thinly sliced

300ml soya yoghurt

2 tbsp dried mint or — Indian trick, this — mint sauce in a jar, or fresh herbs such as mint (traditional), coriander, dill, parsley or tarragon (very Georgian)

Juice of 1 lemon

Fresh mint leaves, to garnish

So many cultures have a refreshing yoghurty dip: raitha for the Indians, tzatziki for the Greeks. Call it what you like, I love this stuff and can eat it for breakfast, in bed, lunch or dinner.

Mix 1 tbsp salt with the cucumber slices and set aside for 30 minutes or longer, then tip away the liquid released. This is a French tip I learnt to make the cucumber crunchy.

Add the soya yoghurt, dried mint or other herbs and the lemon juice, and mix together. Adjust the seasoning if necessary and garnish with fresh mint.

52

(9) Baba Ghanoush

Serves 4—6

3 large, shiny aubergines

1 heaped tbsp tahini

Juice of 1 lemon

2 garlic cloves, very finely chopped

1 tsp ground cumin

2 tbsp good olive oil

2 tbsp Maldon sea salt

Pomegranate seeds or chopped parsley, to garnish

I make the best baba ghanoush in the world. Yes, I'm boasting, but it's the truth. In fact, I challenge anyone in the entire world to a baba ghanoush-off. No kidding.

Char the aubergines on a gas hob, either directly on the flame or in a flat cast-iron pan, or alternatively under the grill or on a bbq. (You can even perch a disposable bbq on your windowsill. Try not to drop it onto someone's head below.) If you don't like any of those options, roast them in the oven at 190°C/ gas mark 5 for 20—30 minutes until the skin is blackened and the aubergines look shrunken inside. I insist upon this charring process because that's what this dish is all about — the smoky burnt taste from the aubergines. Always include a little bit (a couple of inches) of the charred skin in the dip.

Strip the skin off the aubergines, discard the stems and put the flesh in a blender with a little of the charred skin. Add the other ingredients except the garnish, blend, keep tasting and adjust it to your taste. That's fine, you can. I'm not a food deity. You like less salt? Fine. You like more? Go ahead.

Scoop into a dish, garnish with the pomegranate seeds or parsley and serve.

Nut & Seed Mix

Makes a small bowl

2 sheets of nori seaweed

25g pumpkin seeds

25g sunflower seeds

25g sesame seeds

10g linseed

10g hemp seeds

2 tbsp tamari sauce

My daughter loves this. It was a standard recipe throughout her childhood, one of the few 'healthy' things I could get her to eat. Carry it around in a little ziplock bag or sprinkle it over other foods.

Dry-roast the nori sheets in a frying pan for just 5 seconds; you don't want them to start to shrivel. Set aside. Dry-roast all the seeds in the pan, starting with the largest, the pumpkin seeds. Now add the tamari to the pan and stir to coat the nuts and seeds. Crumble in the nori. Keep in a dry, airtight container for weeks.

Cheesy Popcorn

Makes a bowlful

1 movie or a binge-
watch of a Netflix
series

Olive or coconut oil

An unspecified amount
of popping corn

3 tbsp nutritional
yeast

Sea salt

Optional extras:

Sprinkle over some
seaweed, such
as dulse or sea
lettuce

Crumble over some
Crispy Cavolo Nero
or Kale Chips (see
page 45)

Crumble over some
toasted nori
seaweed and black
sesame seeds

- -

Variations:

Did you know you can
pop grains other than
corn? Try popquinoa,
popamaranth (for this
one do not add oil to
the pan), popbulgur,
popbarley, popwildrice
and popsorghum.
However, these grains
do not expand as much
as corn, are much
smaller, cook faster
and don't need the lid
on the pan. All great
for gluten-free peops.

I got this recipe from my Canadian friend, Juanita,
who has lived in France for a couple of decades. She
mentioned measurements by cup and I replied that we
don't use cups in the UK. It's often more difficult
to be accurate with cups rather than weights. Juanita
doesn't stress about accuracy. "I make some lovely
muffins and I don't measure anything. I just dump it in.
It turns out differently every time but it's edible."
This is her benchmark with food — that it's edible.
It's like Roseanne Barr's attitude to raising children:
"As a housewife, I feel that if the kids are still
alive when my husband gets home from work, then hey,
I've done my job."

So this is a very low-stress, Juanita-style recipe.
Movie-time popcorn but with the cheesy, healthy flavour
of nutritional yeast. I can't give you the exact amount
of popcorn kernels to use, as it depends on the size
of your receptacle. You want a single layer of popcorn
to cover the base of the pan. Do try to buy as fresh a
popcorn as you can. I know it's dried, but like rice,
fresher is better. So check those sell-by dates.

■ ■

Take a large, heavy-bottomed saucepan with a
well-fitting lid. Put in enough oil to cover the
base and add 3 or 4 popping corn kernels. Replace
the lid. Turn the heat up to medium-high. When
those 3 or 4 kernels pop, it's time to add the
rest of the popping corn. Put in enough so that
you have one layer covering the base of the pan.
Replace the lid.

After a few seconds, the popping will commence.
Eventually the sound will subside with only
the odd pop. Take off the heat. Open the lid and
add nutritional yeast flakes and salt to taste.
Pour into a bowl. The best bit is when you've
eaten all the popcorn and you wipe the bottom
of the bowl with your finger, retrieving all the
remaining flavourful remnants.

Roasted Chickpeas

Makes a small jar

400g tin of chickpeas,
    drained and rinsed

2 tbsp olive oil

1 tsp ground cumin

1 tsp ground coriander

½ tsp cayenne pepper

1 tsp sea salt

These can be a snack or a topping for soups
and salads. I've also tried this successfully
with soya beans.

Preheat the oven to 160°C/gas mark 2½. Dry
the chickpeas thoroughly using kitchen paper.
Place on a baking sheet lined with a silicone
baking mat, add the oil, spices and salt and
thoroughly mix until evenly coated. Spread
them in an even layer and bake for about
1 hour until crisp. Add more seasoning if
you wish. Leave to cool, then store in a dry,
airtight container for up to 2 weeks.

Energy Balls

Makes 15—20

10 Medjool dates,
    stoned and finely
    chopped

100g crunchy peanut
    butter, or other
    nut butter, at room
    temperature

25g chopped toasted
    pecan nuts or other
    nuts

1 tbsp carob molasses

3 tsp maple syrup

1 tsp vanilla paste

Pinch of sea salt

To coat:

Toasted coconut

Carob/cocoa powder

Vegan dark chocolate
    sprinkles

Finely ground seeds,
    such as pale green
    pumpkin seeds

Ground pistachio nuts

Poppy seeds

Spirulina powder

Crushed pink
    peppercorns

Beetroot powder

Ginseng powder

Edible glitter

These little pick-me-ups
are good to keep in your
pocket or bag. Think:
healthy chocolate truffles.
Make the balls, then coat
them in different powders
of your choice, including
edible glitter for party
occasions or gifts.

Blend the dates, nut
butter and pecans
together in a food
processor, then stir
in the rest of the
ingredients. Set out
small saucers of, say,
3 rolling ingredients
and shape small balls
from the mixture, then
roll them in one of the
coatings, alternating
so that you have a
pretty selection.

Dried Pineapple Flowers

Makes about 10

These are super sweet and pretty. They can be used to decorate cakes or eaten as a snack.

■ ■ ■ ■ ■ ■ ■ ■ ■ ■ ■ ■ ■ ■ ■ ■ ■ ■ ■ ▪

1 pineapple

Gold lustre dust
  (optional)

Preheat the oven to 110°C/gas mark ¼.

Top and tail the pineapple by slicing off the top and bottom. Then stand it on a chopping board (tuck a tea towel underneath to stop it wobbling) and, using a sharp knife, carefully remove the skin with a downwards motion, turning round the pineapple as you work around the sides. Then, with a melon baller or a sharp teaspoon, remove the 'eyes' (the brown spiky circles).

Turn the pineapple on its side and slice as thinly as possible: the thinner the slice, the prettier it will look and the faster it will dry out. Place the slices on a wire rack set over a baking tray (to enable both sides to dry out).

Bake in the low oven for 30—60 minutes or until they are dry and curling up around the edges. Once they are dried, you could brush the edges with gold lustre powder for a pretty effect.

Fruit Leathers

Makes several roll-ups

Like with jam, certain fruits are more suitable than others for fruit leather. For instance, I once tried to make fruit leather from watermelon, which didn't work as well.

Here I used both red and yellow plums. Other fruits that work well include apples, apricots, bananas, berries, cherries, gooseberries (you will need more sugar), mangoes, nectarines, peaches, pears, pineapple, raspberries and strawberries. Some fruits, such as blueberries, you can use in combination with the more suitable fruits. You could also add small amounts of flavouring, such as juice from freshly minced ginger, ground cinnamon or nutmeg, maple syrup, vanilla extract or paste. You could also add seeds to the leather sheets.

If you have a dehydrator, fruit leather is even easier to make.

1kg plums

4 tbsp agave nectar

Juice of ½ lemon

I am lucky enough to have a very powerful blender, a Vitamix, which meant that I didn't have to skin the plums for this recipe. Otherwise, score a cross on the top of each plum with a knife, and leave them for 30 seconds in boiling water. The skin should come off easily. Remove the stones.

Pulse the flesh in a blender, then add the agave nectar and lemon juice. You can use sugar but an inverted sugar such as agave means that there is less chance of crystallisation than with sugar.

Strain the pulp so that there is less juice. For this recipe, I made 2 sheets of 'leather' — one that was strained and one that was not. The unstrained leather was more textural and less smooth but both worked fine. It depends on the fruit. Some fruits have a great deal of juice, so you'd want to strain that out, otherwise you could be drying out the leather for days.

Preheat the oven to 100°C/gas lowest setting and line a flat baking sheet with a silicone baking mat. Using a spatula, spread out the plum purée to about 5mm thick. You want it thin enough to dry out but not so thin that you do not have a 'rollable' leather. So make sure you can't see through the purée and remember that it will contract as it dries.

Put in the very low oven for several hours, checking hourly. If it's not quite dried out when you need to go out or go to bed, turn the oven off after a few hours and leave it (overnight, for example).

When it's sufficiently dried out, carefully peel the leather off the silicone sheet and place it on parchment paper. Cut it into strips and roll it up with strips of the baking parchment. Great for lunchboxes and kids.

Breakfast

A good breakfast sets you
up for the day and means
you are less likely to suffer
from low blood sugar. Here
are a few vegan-friendly
ideas — some are classic,
like muesli or porridge;
others are more exotic,
imaginative replacements
for the full-monty cooked
English breakfast.

Drinks

These drink recipes are nutritionally rich and fulfilling, taste-wise. Great for a quick brekkie on the run. You can even make them the night before and keep in the fridge overnight. A general recipe for nut milk is found on page 29.

For all the recipes below, whizz all the ingredients together, except any garnishes, in a powerful blender such as a Vitamix. (Photo on page 60.)

Mango Lassi

Serves 1

This was a favourite order of mine at Pogo's punk café in Hackney, which held sway for all good animal activists in the noughties. Yes, it was all a bit 'Judean People's Front', with many wars between the freegans, the flexitarians and the vegans. Myself — I was accused of not being quite 'consensual' enough as a chef in the kitchen, i.e. being a non-PC bossy boots. But some of the food was good.

50ml mango purée or pulp

50ml coconut yoghurt (e.g. CoYo)

100ml sweetened soya milk

Seeds of 1 green cardamom pod, ground (¼ tsp)

Handful of ice cubes

Dried mango strips, to garnish

Coconut Smoothie

Serves 1

250ml coconut milk

125ml coconut yoghurt (e.g. CoYo)

½ banana, frozen

2 tbsp agave nectar

Pinch of sea salt

Unsweetened dried coconut shavings, to garnish

Cashew Nut, Banana & Apricot Smoothie

Serves 2

500ml Cashew Nut Milk (see page 29)

1 banana, peeled

2 scoops of dairy-free vanilla ice cream (such as Swedish Glace)

5 dried apricots, soaked in cold water for 30 minutes, then drained

2 tbsp agave nectar

1 tsp vanilla paste

Mexican Chocolate Shake

Serves 2

A little spice to get you going in the morning. Dark chocolate lowers blood pressure and alleviates depression. Cocoa nibs are like amphetamines for the clean living.

350ml oat, almond or hazelnut milk

30g vegan dark chocolate

1 tbsp cocoa nibs (optional)

1—2 tbsp cocoa powder, plus extra to garnish

½ tsp ground cinnamon

2 tbsp agave nectar

½ tsp chipotle paste (optional)

Handful of ice cubes

Mean, Lean & Green Shake

Serves 2

Green juice is all the rage amongst dieters and health freaks. Now that the current advice is to eat '7 a day' (5 vegetables and 2 fruit), you can bust through about half of that in this one green smoothie.

100g seedless green grapes

100g baby spinach, any big stems removed

½ cucumber, peeled

½ avocado, peeled and stoned

100g blueberries, plus extra to garnish

A few sprigs of parsley

Large pinch of alfalfa sprouts

Juice of ½ lemon

200ml water

1 tsp spirulina powder (optional)

Light-as-Air Crumpets

Makes 16

Dare I say it, but these are even lighter and more delicious than standard crumpets. Slather with tahini, agave nectar, Marmite or jam.

....

70g strong white bread flour

70g plain flour

7g fast-action dried yeast

½ tsp sea salt

1 tsp caster sugar

275ml warm almond milk

¼ tsp bicarbonate of soda

100ml warm water

Melted coconut oil, for greasing and cooking

Equipment:

Cast-iron pan or griddle, or good-quality heavy-bottomed frying pan

At least 4 metal crumpet or egg rings or plain metal pastry cutters, about 7.5cm diameter

Heatproof pastry brush

Mix together the flours, yeast and salt in a bowl. Add the sugar and warm almond milk and beat together until you have a smooth batter. Cover and leave to rise in a warm place for 45 minutes.

Mix the bicarbonate of soda into the water, then leave for a couple of minutes before adding it to the batter. Cover again and leave to rest for 20 minutes.

Heat your pan (or griddle) over a medium-high heat. You want it quite hot, but not so hot that the crumpets burn on the outside before they are cooked on the inside. Arrange a little pot of melted coconut oil, the pastry brush and the batter with a small ladle or tablespoon next to the hob.

You'll need to cook your crumpets in batches. Add a little oil to the pan and grease the insides of the metal rings (or cutters) using the pastry brush. Allow the rings to heat up in the pan and then, using the small ladle (or tablespoon), fill each ring to a depth of no more than 2cm (don't overfill them or they will take too long to cook and the holes won't have enough time to form).

Now wait. Be patient. Only turn your crumpets over once the surface is set and lots of holes have appeared through the top of the batter. Then, using tongs or the corner of a tea towel, lift away the rings, flip over the crumpets using a palette knife and continue cooking briefly for a minute or so on the other side. This way you can get a rolling system going, using the empty hot metal rings for the next batch, greasing them with oil as you go (be careful, as the rings will be hot!) and ladling in more batter, while the first batch, having set their shape in the rings, continues to cook. Cook the remaining crumpets in the same way until they are all done.

Transfer the cooked crumpets to a wire rack. To keep them hot, lay them one by one in a large 'envelope' of foil and keep them in the oven on its lowest setting.

Black Cat Pancakes with Bananas, Cinnamon & Maple Syrup

Makes about 8

Carolyn Stapleton is the chef of a vegan restaurant near 'murder mile' in Clapton called the Black Cat on the site of the old Pogo café. She's a fantastic cook!

Here is her recipe for fluffy American-style vegan pancakes.

½ banana, peeled

50g caster sugar

250ml soya or other dairy-free milk

250g self-raising flour

1 level tbsp baking powder

Pinch of sea salt

50ml sparkling water

1 tsp coconut oil (optional)

To serve:

1–2 bananas, peeled and sliced

1 tsp ground cinnamon

Maple syrup

Coconut oil or vegan spread

In a food processor, blend the banana, sugar and half the milk together, then transfer to a stand mixer or a bowl.

Whisk in the flour and remaining milk, then add the baking powder, salt and sparkling water. (I have used sparkling elderflower drink when I didn't have any sparkling water, and this worked fine too!) The thicker the mixture, the thicker and more pillowy your pancakes will be, so aim for a consistency that is just about pourable, something like double cream.

To cook, heat up a flat frying pan or 'crêpière'. You can cook them in a dry pan or just rub it slightly with a little coconut oil. Using a large spoon, ladle in about 2 spoonfuls per pancake. Wait until bubbles start to form before flipping them over. When both sides are golden and pillowy, transfer to a heatproof plate, cover with foil and keep warm in the oven on its lowest setting.

Cook the remaining pancakes in the same way until they are all done. Serve with the sliced banana, cinnamon, maple syrup and coconut oil or vegan spread.

Chirpy Muesli

Makes 1.5kg

125ml nut oil, such as
almond or hazelnut

150ml maple syrup or agave
nectar

1 tsp vanilla extract

500g rolled oats

50g pecan nuts, roughly
chopped

150g hazelnuts, roughly
chopped

75g pumpkin seeds

75g sunflower seeds

50g golden linseed

100g desiccated coconut

300g mixed dried fruit, such
as dates, figs, apricots,
raisins, sultanas,
cranberries, mulberries,
sour cherries, blueberries
(the larger fruit should
be chopped)

To serve:

Soya, rice, oat or nut milk

Fresh fruit, such as sliced
bananas

Here is a good recipe for muesli without
honey. Feel free to change the nuts and
fruit to whatever you happen to have
in your store cupboard. There are so
many seeds and nuts in it (unlike the
forlorn culinary treasure hunt you have
to do with shop-bought) that you might
end up chirping cheerfully like a bird
throughout the morning. I served this at
a pop-up restaurant I ran at Bestival
music festival and people came up to me
saying it was without a doubt the best
muesli they'd ever eaten. This will last
up to 2 months in a dry place.

Preheat the oven to 170°C/gas mark 3.

Put the oil, maple syrup or agave
nectar and vanilla extract in a small
saucepan over a low heat and gently
melt together.

Mix the oats, nuts, seeds and coconut
together in a large bowl. Pour over
the melted oil mixture and stir
really well to ensure all the dry
ingredients are evenly coated.

Divide the mixture between 2 large
baking trays and spread it out in an
even layer. Bake in the oven for 20—
25 minutes, tossing every 5 minutes,
until golden brown. Remove from the
oven and leave to cool on the trays,
stirring every now and then. (If
you transfer it to a deep bowl while
still warm, it will go soggy.)

Once completely cool, transfer to a
large bowl and stir in your choice of
dried fruits. Serve with the dairy-
free milk of your choice and top with
fresh fruit.

Porridge with Rhubarb, Date Sugar & Cardamom Compote

Serves 1

Porridge has so many health benefits that I hardly need mention them. One of the most rewarding aspects of porridge is that you will not feel hungry for at least 4–5 hours after eating it, due to the slow release of complex carbohydrate energy. There are many different toppings for porridge, and this is only one suggestion. If rhubarb is not in season, then simply slice up a few apples and sprinkle with ground cinnamon. Cinnamon is nature's blood sugar regulator.

I love rhubarb, both the tender, crimson forced stems in winter and the thicker, rougher stuff you get in spring (from which you should remove any particularly stringy spines). It is a vegetable, and buckwheat is related to it. Don't eat the leaves, as they are toxic, but keep the leaves on until you are ready to use it.

For the compote:

3 rhubarb stalks, trimmed and cut into 5cm batons

3 tbsp date sugar (or coconut palm or cane sugar), or to taste

3 green cardamom pods, crushed

For the porridge:

50g organic medium oatmeal

300ml oat milk, e.g. Oatly (you can use water or soya milk, but I found Oatly perfectly complements porridge, being made of oats)

Large pinch of sea salt

To make the compote, preheat the oven to 200°C/gas mark 6. Mix the rhubarb, sugar and cardamom in a baking dish, cover with foil and bake for 10–15 minutes. Add more sugar to taste, if necessary.

You could soak the oatmeal overnight in the milk, as this does make a softer gruel. Otherwise, put the oatmeal and the milk into a medium saucepan over a medium-high heat and bring to the boil while stirring. Once the porridge starts to bubble, turn down the heat and simmer for 10 minutes. About 5 minutes before the end, add the salt and keep stirring. Top with the compote, eat and feel satisfied.

Scrambled Tofu on Truffled Sourdough Bruschetta

Serves 4

3—4 tbsp olive oil

2 spring onions, finely
  sliced

6—8 medium brown mushrooms,
  sliced

200g silken tofu, drained
  and crumbled

1 tbsp thyme, oregano or
  marjoram leaves

4 slices of sourdough or
  other good bread

1 garlic clove, halved

Truffle oil or truffle paste

Handful of basil leaves,
  shredded

Sea salt and freshly ground
  black pepper

This is vaguely like scrambled eggs but
not really. It's a very easy, quick
breakfast and can be flavoured any which
way: Mexican, Indian, Italian. The truffle
turns it into a bit of a luxury. Tofu is a
great flavour absorber. For this scramble,
use firm but silken tofu and drain it.
This is one of my favourite dishes in the
book — absolutely delicious.

Heat the oil in a frying pan over a
medium heat and, when hot, sprinkle
in the spring onions, mushrooms,
tofu and herbs. With a spatula, fry
the tofu until it looks dry, like
scrambled eggs. Season with salt and
pepper to taste.

In the meantime, toast the bread,
then rub with the cut garlic clove.
Drizzle over the truffle oil or paste.

Serve both together, with the
shredded basil as a garnish and, if
you like, a couple of turns of fresh
black pepper from the mill.

Tofu Shakshouka

Serves 2

Good slug of olive oil

Half a dozen cherry
tomatoes, cut in half

1 red pepper, deseeded and
cut into thin strips

5 spring onions, preferably
purple, chopped into
rounds, plus extra, sliced
lengthways, to garnish

5 garlic cloves, cut into
slivers

400g tin of chopped tomatoes

1 tbsp sweet paprika

1 tbsp freshly ground
coriander seeds

1 tsp ground cumin

A few saffron strands

1 tsp dried chilli flakes,
or more, to taste

Sea salt, to taste

Scoop of soya yoghurt,
to serve (optional)

400g silken tofu, drained
and cut into cubes (on
your palm — see recipe
introduction, page 106 —
or in the box)

Warm pitta bread, to serve

I visited Israel in 2012, and whatever
you think about the politics, the food
is downright amazing. These people like
to eat and know what to eat. One of the
most popular breakfasts is shakshouka,
which is a dish of eggs cooked in a spicy
red tomato sauce. I visited a vegetarian/
vegan restaurant there called Ornella and
Ella, and I had the tofu shakshouka. I was
supposed to share it with my companion
but it was so delicious that I scoffed
the lot in one sitting. I'm a big fan of
tofu for taking on flavours so willingly.
Silken tofu provides a delightful textural
contrast here.

Heat the oil in a good-quality frying
pan, ideally non-stick. Then add the
cherry tomatoes and the red pepper
strips and fry until slightly golden.
Add the spring onions. Ditto.

Add the garlic, tomatoes, paprika,
ground coriander, cumin, saffron, chilli
flakes and salt. Stir briefly to combine.
Now add the tofu but don't stir,
otherwise you might break it up — it's
delicate. Leave to cook over
a medium-high heat for 20—30 minutes
until all the tomatoes seem cooked
through and the tofu has sort of
poached into a silky wobbliness but
still retains a cube-like shape. Add
some more water or tomato liquid if
the mixture becomes too dry.

Add a quenelle of soya yoghurt, if you
like, and some purple spring onions on
top. Eat with warm pitta. Really, this
is a dish to convince non-veggies.

Quesadillas with Black Beans & Tofu, Huitlacoche & Rajas

Serves 4

I used to live in Los Angeles, where I worked in a photographic lab printing pictures by famous photographers. Every morning a Mexican food truck would pull up at about 11am and I'd order a cheesy green chilli quesadilla. Heaven! At that time I was going to the gym every day doing Jane Fonda-style 'aerobics' — remember them? — so I could afford to eat my body weight in fat 'n' carbs. This is a vegan version, equally tasty but rather healthier. Huitlacoche is a fungus that grows on corn, which I'll admit sounds disgusting but absolutely isn't. (What do you think mushrooms are?) Rajas are tinned strips of poblano chilli, which are very mild but tasty. You can buy huitlacoche and rajas online at Mexican food sites (like www.mexgrocer.co.uk and casamexico.co.uk). They are the authentic taste of Mexican cooking. If you need that cheesy feel, then use one of the stretchier vegan cheeses such as Cheezly, sold in slices. You could also add slices of avocado and soya yoghurt as 'sour' cream.

This is a great recipe for a weekend brunch to share with family or friends. I've got a few ingredients here, so you could lay them all out and mix and match.

Olive oil, for frying

1 onion, diced

1 red pepper, deseeded and thinly sliced

1 jalapeño chilli, deseeded and chopped

1 tbsp chopped garlic

400g tin of black beans (or pinto beans if unavailable), drained

1 litre vegetable stock

Juice of 1 lime

2 tsp ground cumin

50g vegan dark chocolate (optional)

1 chipotle, roasted and then soaked (see page 19)

1 tbsp sweet paprika, plus 1 tsp

1 tbsp fresh or dried thyme leaves

Large handful of chopped coriander leaves

1 tsp ground cumin

A few drops of chipotle or Tabasco sauce

400g firm tofu, drained and sliced 1cm thick

1 small tin of huitlacoche (or mushrooms), drained

Handful of green rajas (or mild green chillies/jalapeños, roasted, deseeded, skinned and cut into strips) from a small tin, plus extra to serve

16 small or 8 large wheat tortillas

Vegan melty cheese, sliced (optional)

Sea salt and freshly ground black pepper

To serve:

Avocado slices

Soya yoghurt

Lime wedges

Coriander leaves

To make the black bean chilli, heat 2 tbsp olive oil in a saucepan over a medium heat and fry the onion until soft, then season with salt and pepper. Add the red pepper, jalapeño, garlic and beans. Continue to fry for a couple of minutes, then add the stock and lime juice. Add the cumin, chocolate, if using, chipotle, the 1 tbsp paprika and thyme leaves. Lower the heat and cook for 30 minutes. Check the seasoning, then remove from the heat, stir in the coriander and set aside in a bowl.

Heat some olive oil in a frying pan, then add the 1 tsp paprika, cumin, 1 tsp salt and chipotle or Tabasco sauce. Add the tofu and fry lightly until warmed through. Add the huitlacoche (or mushrooms) and a few of the rajas (or green chilli) strips, stirring carefully so as not to break up the tofu. Set aside in a bowl.

You will need to cook these in batches, 1–2 at a time depending on the size of the tortillas and your frying pan. Lay out 2 tortillas and spread the black bean chilli in a thin layer, then the tofu mixture. If you have vegan cheese, add that in slices too. Place 2 tortillas over the top, pressing down slightly.

Fry the assembled tortillas in a dry, flat frying pan over a medium heat, flipping them over once the underneath tortilla starts to brown. Once the other side is done, remove from the heat and cut into quarters. Keep hot in a low oven while you repeat with the remaining tortillas until they're all done.

Serve with avocado, soya yoghurt, some more of the rajas, lime wedges and coriander leaves.

Poppy Seed Waffles with Blueberries, Orange Zest & Maple Syrup

Makes 4—8

Soya butter or coconut oil,
    for greasing

For the waffles:

50g caster sugar

1½ tsp baking powder

250g plain flour

250ml hemp or rice milk

75ml coconut oil, melted

1 tsp vanilla paste

2 tbsp poppy seeds

For the blueberry sauce:

150g blueberries

50g sugar

3 tbsp maple syrup, plus
    extra to serve

Pared zest and juice of
    1 orange

Equipment:

Waffle maker

I love poppy seeds; they are basically drugs, a mild form of opium. Remember that episode in *Seinfeld* where Julia Louis-Dreyfus tests positive for heroin? Turns out she was eating too many poppy-seed bagels. So it goes without saying that this is a feel-good recipe, perfect for a weekend brekkie. Trippy.

Heat up your waffle maker and grease with soya butter or coconut oil.

Mix the waffle ingredients together in a bowl.

Put the blueberries, sugar, maple syrup and orange zest and juice in a medium saucepan over a medium-high heat, keeping back a little of the orange zest to serve. Stir until the blueberries start to break down but have not lost their shape entirely. Then take off the heat and set aside.

Ladle just enough of the waffle batter to fill the waffle maker sections, then spread it around. Close the lid and cook for 3—5 minutes, or according to the manufacturer's instructions. Transfer to a heatproof plate, cover with foil and keep warm in the oven on its lowest setting.

Cook the remaining waffles in the same way until they are all done. Serve the waffles hot with the blueberry sauce, a little extra maple syrup and the reserved orange zest.

Lunch

These light dishes are
perfect for lunch. But if
you are throwing a formal
dinner party, you could
make some of these recipes
as starters and follow them
with something from the
Dinner chapter.

Soya Soup with Silken Tofu & Edamame Beans

Serves 4

700ml unsweetened soya milk

10cm piece of kombu

1 heaped tbsp white miso

2 tsp yuzu paste

2 tsp light soy sauce

400g block of silken tofu, drained

75g edamame beans, podded

Sea salt

Japanese nanami togarashi (chilli seasoning), to garnish

A subtle, refreshing and delicate soup. Very clean and fresh tasting.

In a medium saucepan over a very low heat, gently warm the soya milk with the piece of kombu, then take it off the heat and leave to infuse for about 30 minutes.

Return the pan to the heat and add the miso, yuzu paste and soy sauce. Cut the block of tofu into quarters, then cut each quarter in half crossways. Add the slices to the soup and poach them over a low heat for 5—10 minutes. Finally, add the edamame beans, reserving a handful to serve. Season with salt to taste.

Ladle the soup into 4 bowls, with 2 slices of silken tofu in the middle. Fish out the piece of kombu and discard. Sprinkle a few edamame beans on top of the soup and sprinkle with the nanami togarashi.

Zurek Sour Rye Soup

Serves 4–6

Homemade sour rye liquid:

40g dark rye flour

1 litre warm water

2 fresh bay leaves

2 allspice berries

2 garlic cloves, thinly
 sliced

For the soup:

20g dried porcini
 mushrooms

250ml boiling water

75ml olive oil

5 shallots, sliced

4 garlic cloves, thinly
 sliced

750g waxy potatoes, peeled
 and cut into small cubes

15cm celery stick, thinly
 sliced

2 fresh bay leaves

3 allspice berries

1 tsp marjoram or oregano
 leaves

A few sprigs of thyme

5 black or green
 peppercorns

1 litre sour rye liquid,
 strained (see above)

A few shavings of fresh
 horseradish

Sea salt and white pepper

For the garnish:

Fresh porcini, shiitake or
 button mushrooms, thinly
 sliced

1 garlic clove

Handful of dill, finely
 chopped

Sour soups in Eastern Europe are made using fermented rye (or wheat). This is one you have to start 2 days in advance in order to ferment the rye flour, but you can buy the sour liquid known as 'zakwas', a liquid sourdough starter, in Polish and Eastern European food shops. Anything fermented is healthy for the flora and fauna of your gut.

Homemade sour rye liquid:

Put the flour, water, bay leaves and allspice berries in a jar and cover the jar with muslin (it needs access to the air to ferment). Leave in a warm place for 2 days, stirring carefully twice a day. After 2 days, add the garlic. If any sediment forms on the top — which is harmless — scrape it off. Once fermented (it should look a bit bubbly and smell slightly sour), strain it and reserve the liquid.

For the soup:

Rinse the dried porcini of dust, put into a small bowl, pour over the boiling water and set aside to soak.

Heat 50ml of the olive oil in a large, heavy-bottomed saucepan, add the shallots and fry until soft, then add the garlic, potatoes, celery, bay leaves, allspice berries, marjoram or oregano, thyme, peppercorns and 1 tbsp salt. Fry for a few minutes until the potatoes start to colour, then add the sour liquid and the soaked porcini with their soaking liquid.

Bring to the boil, then turn down the heat and simmer for 15–20 minutes until the potatoes are tender and the mushrooms soft. Check the seasoning, adding salt, if needed, and white pepper to taste. If you'd like the soup more liquid, you could add 500ml vegetable or mushroom stock at this stage. Grate in some fresh horseradish and cook for another 20 minutes or so. Remove the bay leaves if you wish. Fry up the fresh mushrooms for the garnish with the garlic in the remaining 25ml olive oil, then serve the soup topped with the fried mushrooms and dill.

Hot & Sour Soup

Serves 6

3—4 tbsp groundnut or vegetable oil

3 garlic cloves, very finely chopped

2.5cm piece of ginger, peeled and grated (I keep mine in the freezer to use as and when)

1 punnet (150g) shiitake mushrooms, sliced

1 punnet (150—200g) brown mushrooms, sliced

2 red chillies, deseeded and thinly sliced

Big glug of rice wine or dry sherry

2 litres hot vegetable stock

4 lime leaves (ideally fresh: grow a kaffir lime plant to always have some around)

40ml light soy sauce

25ml dark soy sauce

50ml Chinese black vinegar

Juice of 4 limes

3 tbsp cornflour mixed with 6 tbsp cold water, OR 250g ramen noodles

100g baby corn, halved lengthways

100g sugar snap peas

A few carrots, finely julienned (optional)

150g silken tofu, drained and cut into 1.5cm cubes (in your palm over the pot)

For the garnish:

1 bunch of spring onions, julienned

Handful of bean sprouts, well washed

Mint and coriander leaves

I served this at The Secret Garden Club supper club that I host monthly with gardener Zia Mays. We try to use the produce that I grow in my garden. This time the theme was herbs — classic, unusual and micro. This hot and sour soup is a bit of a mix between a Thai sour soup and a Chinese one. I found that just the black vinegar wasn't sour enough, so I added lime. A proper Chinese hot and sour soup has jelly ears and bamboo shoots in it. I didn't have any, so this is my bastardised version. Fear not, it was damn good even if not entirely authentic.

It's also very Chinese if all the vegetables are julienned (cut into fine strips) and the tofu precisely cut into squares.

Heat the oil in a large pan and add the garlic, ginger and both types of mushroom. Fry for 5—10 minutes until the mushrooms are golden, then add the chillies and rice wine or sherry. Stir for a couple of minutes.

Add the stock, lime leaves, soy sauces, vinegar and lime juice. Taste for the required balance of heat (chilli), sour (lime and vinegar) and salt (soy sauces). Adjust the balance as needed.

Add the cornflour paste (unless you will be adding noodles later; don't add both or it will be too starchy) and simmer for 30 minutes. Next add the baby corn, sugar snaps, carrots if using, and tofu, with the noodles if you haven't added cornflour.

Simmer for 5 minutes, or longer to cook the noodles, then ladle into bowls and top with the spring onions and bean sprouts, then the herbs.

Sweet Potato & Coconut South Seas Soup

Serves 4

50—75ml vegetable or palm oil

1 red onion, diced

4 garlic cloves, very finely chopped

1 red chilli, deseeded and very finely chopped

5cm piece of ginger, peeled and very finely chopped

1 tsp toasted coriander seeds, freshly ground

1 tsp ground turmeric

Pinch of saffron strands

2 sticks of lemongrass, very thinly sliced

1 red pepper, deseeded and cut into strips

1 large sweet potato, peeled and cut into 4—5cm cubes

2 x 400ml tins of coconut milk

Juice of 1 lime, plus extra to serve

100g spinach

Sea salt

Coriander leaves, to serve

I made a scaled-up version of this soup at music festival Bestival when I did a desert island/pirate/ 18th-century shipboard-inspired pop-up. We had a sea-shanty band, rigging in the tent, napkins made from map fabric ('mapkins'), maps as menus, vintage globes and costumes created especially for the crew. Bawdy singing and rum were the order of the day.

I have to admit, cooking in a field is a challenge. For a start, at festivals, none of the staff want to work much. They want to be out there, having fun with everyone else. Oh, I give long, stern lectures beforehand about how they are getting paid and they must be professional. This lecture never works. Luckily, this is a simple soup to make, so I managed to serve it to 800 people without TOO much sweat.

Heat the oil in a large saucepan over a medium heat, add the onion and cook until softened, then add the garlic, chilli, ginger, ground coriander, turmeric, saffron, lemongrass and 1 tbsp sea salt. Stir well, then add the red pepper and sweet potato and fry until lightly golden around the edges.

Add the coconut milk and lime juice and simmer for 10—15 minutes, adding the spinach just before the end; it will wilt in the heat of the soup. Season to taste with salt.

Ladle into bowls, add more lime juice and the coriander and serve with the sambal below.

Coconut, Lime & Chilli Sambal

Serves 4 as a garnish for the soup

1 fresh coconut

2 fresh red chillies, deseeded and very finely chopped

Juice of 2 limes

Handful of coriander leaves

Sea salt

Open the coconut (see page 18), draining the milk into a glass. Peel off the brown skin. Whack the milk and flesh in a Vitamix or powerful food processor. Add the chillies, lime juice, coriander and salt to taste and process until finely minced.

Tortilla & Squash Blossom Soup

Serves 4–6

This is a big favourite in the United States and Mexico, but you don't see it very much in the UK. Do not be afraid: the high proportion of dried chillies is not spicy, as pasilla and anchos are very mild. They do give a deep, authentic taste to the soup. This is a very Frida Kahlo-esque soup — colourful and floral. I once did a Frida Kahlo-themed supper club and almost every guest arrived with a drawn-on mono-brow.

Only add the flowers towards the end of the cooking, as they just need to wilt in the steam of the soup. But if they are the female courgette flowers, which have a tiny courgette attached, cook them a little longer in the heat of the soup so that the courgette part softens a bit.

You can use courgette flowers or any flowers from squash, but remove the larger stamens from squash flowers. Check the insides for insects. To obtain these flowers, make friends with a gardener or, ideally, grow your own.

5 dried pasilla or ancho chillies

3–5 garlic cloves, unpeeled

Olive or vegetable oil

2 white onions, diced

5 tomatoes, diced

750ml vegetable stock

1–2cm achiote paste (available from Mexican online shops)

10–15 squash or courgette flowers

Juice of 1 lime

Handful of coriander leaves

Sea salt

4–6 corn tortillas, cut into strips and fried, OR blue or white corn tortilla chips, to garnish

Soak the chillies as described on page 19, retaining the red-coloured soaking water.

In the meantime, toast the garlic cloves in a little oil in a frying pan over a low heat until softened — about 15 minutes. Slip off the skins and blend the garlic in a food processor with the drained chillies and a little of the reserved red chilli water.

Fry the onions in some oil in a large saucepan until soft, then add the tomatoes and fry lightly. Add the chilli and garlic mixture and stir well. Then add the stock and achiote paste, taste and add a little salt, depending on how salty your stock is.

Cook for at least 30 minutes over a medium-low heat, stirring from time to time, then add the squash or courgette flowers and lime juice. Check and adjust the seasoning and add the coriander leaves.

Ladle the soup into bowls, top with the fried tortilla strips or chips and serve at once.

Smoky Salmorejo with Basil Oil

Serves 4

8 ripe smoked tomatoes, quartered (or add a few drops of liquid smoke to fresh tomatoes)

2 garlic cloves, peeled

1 baguette, sliced

½ onion

200ml extra virgin olive oil

2 tbsp sherry vinegar

1 tbsp smoked paprika

125g basil leaves, blended with 3 tbsp olive oil

Sea salt and freshly ground black pepper

This is the Madrileño version of the Andalucian gazpacho. If you're confident at cold smoking, you can make your own smoked tomatoes by halving and dehydrating 8 ripe tomatoes in a very low oven for 4–6 hours before cold smoking them.

Place 3 tbsp salt, the tomatoes, garlic, bread and onion in a large bowl and cover with boiling water. Leave for 45 minutes, then drain out the water, squeezing the bread, and keeping back a cup for blending purposes.

Place the drained vegetables and bread in a blender or food processor with the reserved liquid and add the oil, vinegar and smoked paprika. Purée until smooth, then check the seasoning, adding pepper and more salt if necessary. Chill in the fridge — overnight if possible, to allow the flavours to meld.

Serve chilled and garnished with the basil oil alongside a cool glass of dry sherry.

Ajo Blanco with Pickled Green Pepper Relish

Serves 4

For the green pepper relish:

2 green peppers

Olive oil

75ml white wine vinegar

2 tbsp granulated sugar

2 tbsp sea salt

1 tsp drained pickled green peppercorns

1 tbsp drained baby capers

Handful of flat-leaf parsley leaves, to garnish

For the soup:

150g blanched almonds

6 garlic cloves, peeled

100g sourdough breadcrumbs

500ml cold water

2 tsp sea salt

200ml extra virgin olive oil

2—3 tbsp white balsamic or sherry vinegar, to taste

White pepper

A chilled Spanish soup made from almonds and garlic. Simple and pale, but elegantly filling. You'll only need a small portion.

Preheat the oven to 200°C/gas mark 6. To make the green pepper relish, place the green peppers on a baking tray, toss in a little olive oil and roast in the oven for 15—20 minutes until the skin is blackened. Place in a plastic bag for 5 minutes, then strip off the shiny skin and deseed them.

In a small saucepan, combine the wine vinegar, sugar and salt and place over a medium heat until the sugar and salt have dissolved. Remove from the heat and let cool completely.

Tear or slice the peppers into strips and add to the cooled pickling liquid with the peppercorns and capers. Then heat until the vinegar evaporates.

For the soup, briefly toast the almonds in a dry frying pan over a medium-high heat for no more than 1—2 minutes. Tip onto a plate and leave to cool, then process in a blender with the garlic, breadcrumbs, water, salt, olive oil and balsamic or sherry vinegar. Chill in the fridge until ready to serve.

Season the chilled soup with white pepper, then ladle into bowls, place a little green pepper relish in the middle of each and scatter over a few parsley leaves.

Popcorn Chowder with Achiote

Serves 4

I developed this chunky fresh soup for another Bestival menu. People from all over Britain go to Bestival but pass rapidly through the picture-perfect countryside, which is a shame because the Isle of Wight has some of the best ingredients in Britain. With this recipe I was attempting to somehow bring the Isle of Wight back into the festival by using local seasonal ingredients. I got this corn from farmer Ben Brown from Arreton, just a mile down the road from the festival. The corn was so sweet you could eat it raw, straight from the cob, like sugar.

I served this in soup bowl-sized pumpkins, again from Ben Brown, oiled, salted and lightly roasted prior to filling them with soup.

4 little pumpkins, the size of bowls

Corn or vegetable oil

2 fresh corn cobs

1 small onion, diced

1 garlic clove, very finely chopped

2cm achiote paste (available from Mexican websites)

1–2 whole chipotle chillies in adobo sauce (depending on your heat tolerance), finely diced

3 tbsp cornmeal or masa harina (NOT cornflour)

450ml hot vegetable stock

300ml soya cream

1 tsp sweet smoked paprika, plus extra to garnish

Sea salt

For the garnish:

100g popping corn

A little corn oil

Handful of coriander leaves, to garnish

Preheat the oven to 200°C/gas mark 6.

First prepare the pumpkins. Slice off the top (which will be the lid), then hollow out the centre, leaving enough flesh inside the skin so that the soup will not leak. Discard the insides. Oil the outside of the pumpkin bowls and lids, rub sea salt inside and out and roast for 15–20 minutes. Leave to cool.

Grasp each corn cob firmly upright and slice downwards on each side using a sharp knife; the kernels should fall away easily.

Sweat the onion in a large pan in some oil, then add the garlic, achiote paste and corn. Lightly sauté, then add the chipotle and stir well. Add the cornmeal or masa harina, hot stock, soya cream, 2 tsp salt and the smoked paprika. Check and adjust the seasoning.

Bring to the boil, then simmer for at least 20 minutes. This soup does deepen in flavour if you keep it going. I mention a minimum here, but I often feel soup is better the next day.

Meanwhile, put the popping corn and a little corn oil in a large saucepan with a well-fitting lid and place over a high heat. Once the popping subsides, leave behind the unpopped kernels and season the rest with sea salt and the sweet smoked paprika.

Ladle the hot soup into the pumpkin bowls, top with a few coriander leaves and some popcorn and serve.

Peruvian Purple Potato
Papa a la Huancaína

Serves 4

I spent three months in Peru, one of the world's most interesting countries. Unlike most tourists, I spent some time up in the north, at a place called Kuelap, a first-century ruined city at the top of a remote hillside. Rumour has it that tall white people inhabited it, possibly Vikings. This is way before the Spanish arrived and hundreds of years before the Incas.

This Peruvian dish is from a little-visited inland town, Huancayo, to which you can take a train from Lima. It's one of the highest-altitude train rides, almost 5,000 metres in places, in the world. When I embarked upon this journey, 25 years ago, it looked like a bus or tram on a very narrow train track. The back of the carriage was stored with oxygen tankards in case people could not cope with the thin air.

Ideally, this classic Peruvian recipe uses yellow chillies (aji amarillo), but they aren't easy to get hold of. I used an online resource (www.vivaperu.co.uk), but you can substitute with any fruity, pale chilli sauce.

Use the best potatoes you can buy: most impressively, purple potatoes such as Purple Majesty by Albert Bartlett, or rich, waxy yellow Yukon Gold potatoes, or a mixture of both.

4 large purple potatoes, unpeeled

1 tsp aji amarillo paste (see introduction)

1 garlic clove, very finely chopped

250ml soya cream

2 tbsp nutritional yeast

Juice of ½ lime

Sea salt

To garnish:

Lime wedges

Sprigs of coriander

Put the potatoes into a large saucepan, cover with boiling water, add 1 tbsp salt and cook over a high heat. Purple potatoes cook a lot more quickly than white, in maybe half the time, so keep an eye on them. Once the potatoes are cooked, drain and leave to cool. Then slip off the skins and cut into 1.5cm slices.

Meanwhile, put the aji amarillo paste, garlic, soya cream, nutritional yeast, lime juice and 1 tsp salt into a blender and process until smooth. Pour into a small saucepan and heat until warmed through and slightly thickened.

To plate up: first pour the sauce onto the plate, then add the purple potato slices. Garnish with lime wedges and coriander and serve.

Salmagundy

This is a tall layered salad, popular in the 18th century. Hannah Glasse mentions it in her 1747 book, *The Art of Cookery Made Plain and Easy*. I served it at a Soil Association pop-up in Toynbee Hall in London's Tower Hamlets, in a wood-panelled banqueting room. This is not a strict recipe as such; more a compilation of things you can put in it. It's spectacular when done right. If you have a garden, add stalks of herb flowers and edible flowers to turn it into an extravagant display. Who says vegan food is dowdy? Not done like this it isn't. Serve it with dips from the Snacks chapter.

You want height on this dish; you could do individual portions in tea cups, then invert them, or use a bowl or a ring mould for cake. Or just construct it gradually, like a piece of architecture, shaping the vegetables to fit, inserting sprigs as you go, alternating colours and textures. Or you can pop the dips in little cut-glass bowls on a large silver tray, stuffing the surroundings with a burgeoning garden-like salad. This is an eye-popping, wow-inducing centrepiece like a fresh savoury croquembouche.

Romaine lettuce leaves

Red and white endive

Rocket

Watercress

Fennel, thinly sliced, keeping the fronds on

Sorrel leaves

Cucumber slices

Tomatoes, carved like flowers or roses if you have the time

Carrot batons

Red pepper batons

Cauliflower florets

Broccoli florets

Wild asparagus stems

Sage leaves, both plain and variegated

Cornflowers

Nasturtiums

Lavender sprigs

Pea shoots

Chive lengths, if possible with purple flowers if in season

Parsley stalks, curly

Red radishes, decoratively cut

Shallots, finely diced

Strawberries

Hazelnuts

Green olives stuffed with red pepper or lemon

Borage flowers

Dill fronds

Pumpkin seeds

For the classic Dijon mustard dressing:

50ml extra virgin olive oil

1 heaped tbsp Dijon mustard

1 garlic clove, very finely chopped

Juice of ½ lemon

1 tsp sea salt

¼ tsp white pepper

Prep all your vegetables and construct your salad. Whisk the salad dressing ingredients together until they are emulsified. Serve together.

Mosaic of Beetroot & Radish with Horseradish Dressing

Serves 6–8

From the extravagant to the simple; you'll need a mandolin for this or a steady hand and a sharp knife. The slimmer the slices, the prettier this plate can be. If you can find multi-coloured radishes in white, pink, red, purple and black, all the better. Radishes were originally black, then bred to be red; same with carrots, which were originally purple and then bred to be orange — something to do with the royal family in the Netherlands.

100g caster sugar

2 tbsp sea salt

200ml red wine vinegar

2 red beetroots, peeled

2 golden and/or pink beetroots, peeled

150g multi-coloured radishes, very thinly sliced

For the dressing:

50ml of the drained beetroot pickling juice (see above)

50ml olive oil

1 tsp sea salt

5cm fresh horseradish root, peeled and finely grated, or a smear of wasabi paste

2 tbsp poppy seeds

For the garnish:

30g nibbed pistachio nuts

Seeds of ½ pomegranate

In a medium saucepan, heat the sugar and salt with the vinegar until dissolved. Then add the whole beetroots and enough water to cover them. Cook over a medium-low heat for 40 minutes or until tender.

Remove the cooked beetroots from the cooking liquid using a slotted spoon and set aside to cool, reserving the liquid. Put half the radish slices in some of the beetroot cooking juices. After half an hour, they will be pink.

Cut the cooled beetroots into fine slices. Arrange some in overlapping layers in the middle of a large, round plate. Arrange the radish slices and remaining beetroot slices in concentric circles around the plate.

Mix the dressing ingredients together and drizzle over the salad. Dot with bright green pistachio nibs and blood-red pomegranate seeds.

Green Papaya & Courgette Fettuccine with Thread Noodles & Cashews

Serves 4

120g thread noodles

2 courgettes, julienned

1 green papaya, peeled, deseeded and julienned

Handful of cashew nuts, lightly toasted

1 red chilli, very finely chopped

1 garlic clove, very finely chopped

4cm piece of ginger, peeled and very finely chopped

1 tbsp palm sugar

1 tbsp soy sauce

Juice of 1 lime

3 tbsp groundnut oil

Mint and coriander leaves

Sea salt

We can learn from everyone's diet, even if it is not one we would want to follow on a permanent basis. Using raw vegetables to make 'fettuccine' is a trick from the raw food/paleo songbook, a carb-free diet.

For this you will need either a julienne peeler or a machine called a 'spiraliser'. Raw-food-arians love their spiraliser machines! With these, all kinds of vegetables can be turned into noodle-thin strands that you can eat instead of pasta. Like the Chinese, I like to incorporate different textures into my food.

Soak the thread noodles in hot, salted water for 15 minutes, then drain well.

Mix the courgette, papaya, noodles and cashews together. Make the dressing by pounding together, with a pestle and mortar or in a blender, the chilli, garlic, ginger, sugar and soy sauce. Add the lime juice and oil and stir into the courgette, papaya and noodles. Garnish with mint and coriander leaves and serve.

Lettuce Cups with 'Ceviche' & Sweet Potato

Serves 4–6

Palm hearts have a similar structure and texture to crab sticks. Use these for a 'ceviche' salad in Baby Gem leaves. Also good as a canapé before dinner. When I was travelling in Peru, I often had ceviche at roadside stalls, served with a sweet potato. The starchiness perfectly complemented the citrusy ceviche. I'd use it to mop up the juices. (Photo on page 76.)

2 large sweet potatoes, peeled

2 Baby Gem lettuces, leaves separated

400g tin of hearts of palm, drained and rinsed

¼ red onion, finely diced

10cm celery stick, finely sliced into little crescents

2 cherry tomatoes, thinly sliced

1 jalapeño or green chilli, deseeded and very finely chopped

Juice of 1 lime

1 tsp sweet paprika

50ml Vegan Mayonnaise (see page 32)

1 ripe avocado, peeled, stoned and diced

Sea salt

Handful of coriander leaves, to serve

Boil the sweet potatoes in salted water in a medium saucepan for about 20 minutes until cooked. Drain and leave to cool, then cut into quarters.

Pick out the baby gem lettuce leaves that form a little bowl rather than the tiny leaves at the end, and arrange on a serving dish or plate.

Slice the hearts of palm in half lengthways, then cut into 5mm crescents. Put into a bowl and add the onion, celery, tomatoes and chilli. Season with some of the lime juice, the paprika and salt to taste. Add the vegan mayonnaise and mix well. Finally, add the avocado and squeeze over some more lime juice.

Scoop the ceviche into the lettuce leaves and arrange the sweet potatoes on the serving dish or plate. Scatter with the coriander and serve.

Pomelo, Chilli, Peanut & Coriander Salad

Serves 2

1 pomelo, peeled and segmented

1 small red onion, finely sliced

3 spring onions, sliced into thin rounds

50g peanuts, crushed

Handful of coriander leaves

Handful of mint leaves

Handful of Thai sweet/holy basil leaves (optional)

For the dressing:

50ml groundnut oil

20ml sesame oil

Juice of 2 limes

1 red bird's eye chilli, deseeded and finely diced

2 tsp sugar

1 tsp sea salt

2cm piece of ginger, peeled and very finely chopped

I have a slight obsession with citrus — it's so much more interesting than oranges and lemons. Recent discoveries I've made within the citrus family include Meyer lemons (hard to get hold of in the UK), Bengali limes (large, green knobbly fruit), bergamot (used in Earl Grey tea), pomelos and yuzu (fresh yuzu is impossible to source in the UK, but now we can get the juice or the purée). Some of these fruits are fragrant, and just one will transform a dish. I always nab a few blood oranges or Seville bitter oranges, in season in January, for gorgeous crimson-bleeding salads or to make my yearly marmalade. With a citrus salad one tends to go a bit Asian, but there is also the classic Italian combination of Sicilian blood orange and thinly sliced fennel.

Pomelos are enormous grapefruit-style fruits that you can often buy in Asian shops. If you can't get hold of one, feel free to use pink grapefruit, of which you can now buy sweet cultivars. This is very refreshing.

First dot the pomelo segments around the plate, then add the rest of the ingredients. Whisk together the dressing ingredients and pour it over the salad.

Vietnamese Summery Rolls

Makes 8

100g vermicelli rice noodles

10 round rice-paper wrappers (includes 2 extras so that you can practise!)

16 button mushrooms, each sliced into 4 thin slices

12—16 baby lettuce leaves

½ cucumber, cut into thin, 4cm-long batons

2 carrots, peeled and cut into thin, 4cm-long batons

3 spring onions, halved lengthways and cut into 5cm sections

100g bean sprouts or alfalfa sprouts

Handful each of coriander and mint leaves

Handful of Thai sweet/holy basil leaves (or ordinary basil)

1—2 red chillies, finely diced

Borage flowers, cornflowers (pink or blue) and marigold petals

For the dipping sauce:

50ml soy sauce

Squeeze of lime juice

Options: instead of rice wrappers, you can use sturdy salad leaves such as Swiss chard with the above fillings, or with more Westernised fillings like hummus (see page 47) with julienned carrots or radishes.

These crunchy, fresh herby rolls from Vietnam are great picnic standbys, particularly if you have gluten-free guests. Think of them as little transparent windows of goodness. The bottom layer of filling, which will be turned over when finished, should be artfully arranged, as it will be visible through the wrapper. Once you get the hang of rolling them up, you'll return to this recipe regularly. On the shoot, food stylist Alice had the idea of adding delicate edible flowers, like eating a summer garden.

Soak the rice noodles in boiling water for 5—10 minutes until soft, then drain and cool.

Set up an assembly line, with several small bowls for the filling ingredients, and one large bowl of hot water to soak the rice wrappers, with 1 or 2 soaking at a time. Lay a clean tea towel on the work surface.

Take one soaked, soft rice wrapper and lay it carefully on the tea towel. Place 8 mushroom slices in a row, one-third of the way up the rice wrapper, leaving a space at either end for folding.

Taking care not to overfill the roll, add 1 or 2 baby lettuce leaves, then a couple of batons of cucumber and carrot, and some spring onions and bean sprouts or alfalfa. Add some herbs and a few strands of rice noodles. Sprinkle the diced chilli on the rest of the rice wrapper, along with a few pretty leaves and the edible flowers.

Fold over the sides into the centre, then roll up tightly, gathering in as you go and folding in the ends, finally rolling the whole thing into a cylindrical shape. Place seam side down, so they aren't touching, and cover with clingfilm until you have assembled them all.

For the dipping sauce, mix the ingredients together. Arrange the summery rolls on a serving dish and dip in the sauce.

Plantain Fritters with Coconut & Coriander Dip

Serves 6–8

I used to hang out with squatters in Hackney, east London. They often used to 'skip' food, or go 'dumpster diving' as it's called in the States. I was living in the London Fields lido swimming pool. Squatters get a bad rep, but actually they keep buildings alive. The London Fields lido was going to be turned into a car park by Hackney Council, but the squatters stayed there, heated it, repaired it and, when the council said they were going to turn it back into a swimming pool, left peaceably.

It was great fun living in the middle of a beautiful London park. There was a street full of squatters, all of whom had lived in these abandoned houses for longer than 12 years. This meant that they had the right to stay there. (The law has changed now.) I used to visit a local squatter family with my daughter. They were very alternative: home-schooled their kids, refused to have a car, made their own wine and alcohol, grew their own weed, cooked from scratch and ate very good food. They even roasted their own coffee from green beans obtained from Ethiopia. Rob, the husband, made this dish, which I loved. He'd cycle to the local Ridley Road market where Caribbean food was sold.

Make sure you buy ripe — that is, yellow — plantains, not green. Normal bananas won't work, as their texture isn't as sturdy.

2 large, ripe yellow plantains, peeled

1 green chilli, finely sliced

3 tbsp plain flour

50g coriander leaves

Rice bran oil, for deep-frying

Sea salt

For the dip:

1 fresh coconut

1 green chilli, finely sliced

Juice of 2 lemons

Thumb of ginger, peeled and very finely chopped

50g coriander leaves

Mash the plantains by hand or in a food processor. Add the chilli, flour, coriander and some salt.

For the dip, prepare the coconut as described on page 18. Using a powerful blender such as a Vitamix, process the coconut flesh and milk, chilli, lemon juice, ginger, coriander and some salt.

Heat about 1–2cm oil in a deep frying pan. You can use any vegetable oil but rice bran oil is very good with this recipe. Prepare a bowl with kitchen paper to absorb the oil. When a crumb dropped into the oil sizzles, the oil is hot enough. Use a tablespoon to scoop the plantain mixture into the oil. Continue until you have run out of room in the pan or until the mixture is used up. After a few minutes, turn over the fritters. When both sides are golden brown, remove to the kitchen paper to drain. Serve hot with the dip.

Cumin & Onion Farinata

Serves 4–6 (makes 3)

Farinata is a gluten-free, thick pancake made with gram flour, or chickpea flour. In the south of France, you may know it as 'socca'. I first had it in Turin when I attended a Pink Bloc tactical frivolity protest against Berlusconi.

It wasn't all political action though, because, being at heart a *bourgeoise gourmande*, I managed to include some activities such as tasting the ice creams of several gelaterias, attending a chocolate festival in the centre of town and trying the fudgy slices of farinata sold at the local bakery. Which was a useful foodstuff, as half the London samba band were either coeliac, vegan or freegan. I made the farinata with onions and cumin to give it a slightly Middle Eastern vibe. Combined with tabbouleh, it made for a light and healthy weekend lunch.

400g gram (chickpea) flour

300ml water

140ml olive oil

1 tbsp ground cumin

1 tbsp sea salt

2 onions, finely sliced

Olive oil, for frying

Mix the gram flour, water and 50ml of the olive oil together and leave for 2–12 hours, or overnight. Add the cumin and salt.

Cook the onion slices in 50ml of the olive oil in a frying pan over a low heat until caramelised. This will take at least 15–20 minutes. Tip onto a plate.

Preheat the grill to hot. You will need an ovenproof frying pan, ideally cast iron. Even more ideally, you will have 2 of these, so that you can make 2 farinata at once!

Heat a little of the remaining olive oil in the frying pan and add enough batter to cover the bottom of the pan so that it is about 1.5cm thick. Add the caramelised onions and, once the bottom seems done, or set, place the whole frying pan under the hot grill.

Leave until brown on top and slightly crispy at the edges. You can then start on the second one, using a little more oil to grease the pan first.

Cut the farinata into slices like a pizza to serve.

Canary Island-Style Tempero
Salt-Baked Mini Potatoes

Serves 4–6

500g Highland Burgundy
    potatoes

500g Salad Blue potatoes

500g Mayan Gold potatoes

1kg tempero salt (see
    page 19), rock salt or
    sel gris

**For the tofu and pink
pepper cream:**

200g silken tofu, drained

50g cashew nuts

1 preserved lemon, finely
    chopped

1 tsp sea salt

To serve:

1 tbsp pink peppercorns

Balsamic caviar pearls
    (optional)

Baking things on salt is very Spanish. It has
the effect of wrinkling the skins, making the
inside very fluffy and the outside very crispy,
and at the same time seasoning the potato.

I used small heritage potatoes from Carroll's
(www.heritage-potatoes.co.uk), where you can
buy 1.5kg bags of red potatoes such as Highland
Burgundy and blue potatoes such as Salad Blue,
which have brightly hued interiors. In fact,
you could have a very patriotic dish if you
combined it with a white potato such as Golden
Wonder or Mayan Gold. Some of these varieties
are in season from October onwards, but the
rest of the year you could use purple Albert
Bartlett potatoes, which are purpley-blue
inside, and red-skinned potatoes, which are
white in the interior.

This can be a light lunch, served with salad,
or a canapé before dinner.

Preheat the oven to 200°C/gas mark 6.
Wash the potatoes, leaving the skins on,
then dry them. Spread the salt into a
roasting tin. Arrange the potatoes on
the salt, pricking each one, and bake for
45 minutes.

To make the tofu and pink pepper cream,
mix all the ingredients together in a
blender. If you want it thicker, put into
a muslin and let it drain.

Remove the roasting tin from the oven and,
with a knife, cut a slit down the top of
the skin of each potato. Put a quenelle or
scoop of tofu cream onto each potato, with
a few pink peppercorns and some balsamic
pearls, if using, on top. Serve hot on the
bed of salt.

Agedashi Tofu in Broth

Serves 4

400g silken tofu,
   drained

150g cornflour

½ tsp fine sea salt

½ tsp finely ground
   white pepper

Oil, preferably
   groundnut, for
   deep-frying

For the tentsuyu sauce:

300ml dashi
   (see page 28)

4 tbsp soy sauce

3 tbsp sake

2 tbsp mirin

1 tbsp sugar

To serve:

10cm piece of daikon
   radish, peeled and
   grated

Thumb of ginger, peeled
   and grated

2 spring onions, green
   part only, thinly
   sliced

This is one of my favourite Japanese dishes: fried silken tofu in a delicate broth. The Japanese technique for cutting silken tofu is to put it in your hand and cut it directly on the palm.

Cut the tofu into 5—6cm cubes. Blot each piece with kitchen paper. Season the cornflour with the salt and pepper and toss the tofu cubes in it to coat. Set aside.

Place all the ingredients for the tentsuyu sauce in a small saucepan and simmer over a low heat. Do not let it boil.

Heat up the oil for deep-frying in a wok or a deep frying pan. The oil is ready when a cube of bread dropped in rises to the surface and turns golden after about 1 minute. Deep-fry the tofu squares for about 6 minutes until they turn pale golden or crispy. Remove with a slotted spatula and place on a plate lined with kitchen paper.

To serve, place a few pieces of tofu in a small bowl and pour some tentsuyu sauce around the tofu. Top with the grated daikon, ginger and spring onions. Serve immediately.

3 Kinds Of Slider With All The Fixin's

Serves 8—12

The variety of recipes for veggie burgers is never-ending but generally requires some kind of pulse. Buy buns and squares of vegan melty cheese. Make sure you have Pink Pickled Onions (see page 14), relishes and ketchup too.

Classic Bean Slider

Makes 8 sliders or 4 large burgers

400g cooked beans (kidney beans are a good choice)

80g panko or sourdough breadcrumbs

2 tbsp olive oil

2 chia or flax 'eggs' (see page 21)

1 tbsp English mustard

1 tbsp nutritional yeast

Handful of chopped parsley

Squeeze of lemon juice

Oil, for frying

Sea salt and freshly ground black pepper

To assemble:

See Smoked Tofu Slider (page 108)

Preheat the oven to 180°C/gas mark 4.

Combine all the ingredients and form into 8 sliders or 4 large burgers. In an ovenproof frying pan, fry on each side in a little oil, until slightly golden. Transfer to the oven and cook for 7—10 minutes for sliders or 12—15 minutes for burgers. Warm the burger buns in the meantime.

Assemble as for the Smoked Tofu Slider (see page 108).

Sweet Potato Falafel Slider

Makes 10—12 sliders or 6—8 large burgers

1 sweet potato (approx. 250g), skin on

4 garlic cloves, unpeeled

400g tin of chickpeas, or 100g dried chickpeas, soaked overnight

2 tsp coriander seeds, ground

2 tsp cumin seeds, ground

1 onion, diced

2 green chillies, deseeded and finely chopped

Handful of flat-leaf parsley, leaves chopped

Handful of coriander, leaves chopped

Sea salt and freshly ground black pepper

Pitta breads

Tahini

Slices of cucumber

Slices of red onion

Chilli sauce

Preheat the oven to 200°C/gas mark 6. On a baking tray, roast the sweet potato for 30—40 minutes, adding the garlic 15 minutes before the end. Then remove from the oven and let cool. Skin the sweet potato and garlic cloves. Reduce the oven temperature to 180°C/gas mark 4.

Put the drained chickpeas, spices, onion, chillies, herbs and 1 tbsp salt in a food processor, with pepper to taste. (I find a blender like a Vitamix makes the mixture too smooth and fine-grained for falafel.) Process until combined, then form the mixture into 10—12 sliders or 6—8 large burgers and place on a silicone baking mat.

Bake for 15—20 minutes for sliders or 20—30 minutes for burgers, flipping them halfway through. Warm the pitta breads.

Assemble each by adding 1 tbsp tahini, some cucumber and red onion slices, the falafel slider and chilli sauce.

Smoked Tofu Slider

Makes 12 sliders or 6 large burgers

100g sunflower seeds

50g pumpkin seeds

100g stale bread, made into breadcrumbs

1 garlic clove, peeled

225g smoked tofu, drained

100g pack of firm tofu

1 tbsp vegetable stock powder

1 tbsp soy sauce

½ tsp thyme leaves

½ tsp white pepper

Oil, for frying

Sea salt

To assemble, for each patty:

1 burger bun

1 scoop of Vegan Mayonnaise (see page 32)

1 large lettuce leaf (Cos or Romaine)

1 large slice of tomato

1 vegan cheese slice

Couple of slices of sweet pickled cucumber

Ketchup

Preheat the oven to 180°C/gas mark 4.

Put the seeds, breadcrumbs and garlic into the bowl of a food processor fitted with an S-blade and process until the mixture is coarsely ground but still retains some texture (it's okay to see a few whole sunflower seeds in there).

Add the remaining ingredients except the oil, and process until the mixture comes together. Don't process for too long; you want to keep some texture from the seeds. Form into 12 sliders or 6 large burgers (this is easier if your hands are wet).

Heat a little oil in a frying pan, add the sliders and fry on both sides until golden. Warm the buns in the meantime.

Split the buns, add the 'vegannaise', then the lettuce leaf, tomato slice, patty, cheese slice, the pickle and some ketchup. Top with the other bun half and serve.

Onion Rings

Serves 6

This is a side for your sliders. I love sides; I could have a whole meal of sides. I have meat-eating mates who apologise to me when we go to restaurants because I can 'only' have the sides from the menu. Typically meat-centric way of thinking. I'm happy with sides. Really, tapas are sides; small plates are sides. Long live sides.

1 litre vegetable oil, for deep-frying

160g tempura flour

160ml cold sparkling water

150g cornflakes

1 tbsp sweet smoked paprika

1 tbsp sea salt

1 large onion, sliced into 5mm thick rings

Chipotle Vegan Mayonnaise (see page 32) or ketchup, to serve

Heat the oil in your deep-fat fryer to 190°C. In a bowl, combine the flour and sparkling water without over-stirring; the odd lump is fine. Crush the cornflakes so that they resemble large breadcrumbs, then mix with the paprika and salt. Dip each onion ring into the batter mixture, then into the cornflakes. Deep-fry in batches until golden and crispy.

Dip into Chipotle Vegan Mayonnaise or ketchup and serve.

Ramen Hacks

Serves 1

Sometimes when I can't be bothered to cook I buy Pot Noodles. They're quick, they're easy. But, buy good-quality packet noodles; I have it on good authority that the best instant noodles are made by the Koreans. They are 'bouncier'. I chuck out the little packets of powdered vegetable/MSG and sesame oil, make a quick stock and do my own toppings. Here are a few ideas.

Ramen originally derived from Chinese cooking, but took off in Japan after the First World War only after being made less Chinese and more Japanese, adding miso and making it less greasy, more delicate. Ramen is almost like a religion in Japan; everybody has their favourite noodle shop. Check out a very funny 1980s Japanese film called *Tampopo* to find out more. Today, ramen are called 'doll' noodles by many Chinese, as the first manufacturers had a picture of a Japanese doll on the packet. In Japan, they are now bringing out 'feminine' ramen with less salt and MSG, as the biggest consumers are men aged between 20 and 40. Lazy so-and-sos!

----

1 1 packet of ramen

2 Boiling water

3 Own stock, adding one of the following:

2 tbsp mushroom miso (kinoko)

2 tbsp miso

1 tbsp vegetable stock powder

4 Add one or all of these flavourings:

1 tbsp sesame oil

1 tbsp soy sauce

½ tsp finely chopped garlic

2cm piece of ginger, peeled and very finely chopped

½ tsp Sichuan peppercorns, ground

1 tbsp black bean sauce

Squeeze of lime

5 Then add one or more of these toppings:

Small handful of shredded Chinese cabbage

2–3 stalks of Chinese greens, such as bok choi

4–5 baby spinach leaves

Handful of sliced mushrooms, such as shiitake

3–4 slices of tofu, firm, smoked or silken

1 tbsp peanuts

5–6 strips of nori seaweed

Small handful of bean sprouts

2–3 spring onions, chopped

2 tbsp bamboo shoots, fermented (menma)

6 Finish with one or more of these garnishes:

Handful of coriander leaves

Large pinch of pickled ginger

2 tbsp Baechu Kimchi (see page 23)

1 tbsp sesame seeds

Place the ramen into a largeish ceramic or wooden bowl. Pour boiling water onto your stock base, then pour this over the ramen. Add the flavourings. Then add the toppings. Leave for a few minutes until the ramen is soft. Add the garnish.

Mini Bunny Chows

Serves 4–6

5 peaches, not too
    ripe

Coconut or vegetable
    oil, for frying

1 tbsp mustard seeds

1 cinnamon stick

1 bay leaf

5 green cardamom pods

2 cloves, ground

1 tsp ground cumin

1 tsp coriander seeds

1 large onion, diced

3 garlic cloves, very
    finely chopped

Thumb of ginger,
    peeled and very
    finely chopped

1 red chilli, finely
    sliced

1 tbsp ground
    turmeric

100g creamed coconut

350ml hot water

10 small red
    potatoes, skin on,
    quartered

3 tomatoes, roughly
    chopped

½ red pepper,
    deseeded and
    sliced

50g sultanas

4–6 crusty rolls

Handful of coriander
    leaves

1 lime, cut into
    quarters

Sea salt

Bunny chow is similar to the trenchers that medieval Britons used. Prior to the generalised use of cutlery, trenchers were carriers for food and made from stale hollowed-out loaves. The advantage being that once a sauce had softened the bread, you could supplement the dish by tearing off and eating some of the trencher.

Bunny chow is a South African street food, specifically from Durban, and part of its 'rainbow cuisine', with influences from indigenous tribal cooking, Malaysian, British, Afrikaans/Dutch and Indian food. It is filled with a curry. I served mini bunny chows at my South African supper club as a starter. It's a bit like a curry sandwich, very moreish and a great lunch option.

The piece of bread that remains from the hollowing-out process is referred to as a 'virgin'. Most bunnies are made from the ends of a quarter loaf of bread, but ones made from the middle of the loaf, without a crust at the bottom, are called 'funny bunnies'.

Cut a cross in the top of each peach and blanch in boiling water for 1 minute. Peel, remove the stone and cut into small dice.

Heat some oil in a medium saucepan over a medium heat. First sling in the mustard seeds and wait until you hear them pop. Add the cinnamon, bay, cardamom, cloves, cumin and coriander. The secret to a good curry is a mix of whole and ground spices. Here you are tempering them, i.e. frying them a bit before you add the rest of the ingredients, but only slightly, as you don't want everything to taste bitter.

Add the onion, garlic, ginger, chilli and turmeric. Then dissolve the creamed coconut in the hot water and stir into the curry. Add the potatoes and cook for 10 minutes. Add the tomatoes and red pepper, then the peaches and sultanas, with salt to taste.

Cut the tops off the rolls and gut them, pulling out the centres. Scoop the curry inside, scatter over coriander leaves and squeeze lime juice over. Put the cap back on. Eat while looking outside the window at the rain and think of Africa. Also very good the next day!

Dinner

This chapter contains more
substantial meals for
evenings, dinner parties,
special occasions and
weekends. The recipes range
from complicated, for those
of you who want a challenge
and have some time to try
new techniques, to simple,
throw-together meals.
Vegan food is ethical,
inspirational, colourful,
cruelty-free and, above all,
delicious. Here is the proof
of concept.

Fluffy Couscous

Serves 2–4

250g wholewheat couscous

1–2 tbsp sea salt

1 cup of warm water

1 tsp ground ginger

1 tsp coriander seeds

1 tsp ground cumin

1 chilli

4–5 dates or dried apricots, torn into pieces

1 tbsp coconut oil

20g nibbed pistachio nuts

20g dried or semi-dried barberries

2 tbsp black poppy seeds

1 tsp ground cinnamon

1 tbsp rosewater

30ml oil, ideally argan, for its subtly nutty taste

10g bitter orange peel (optional)

Handful of pomegranate seeds (optional)

This is a step-by-step guide to the best way of making couscous. It's a bit fiddly and requires that you eschew such blasphemies as quick-cook couscous. But with this method, each grain will lift and separate just like a Playtex bra. No clumps, no sogginess. So, this weekend, have a go at making couscous from Northern Africa. I've combined it here with spices, and sweet and sour flavours. The idea is to reproduce that Middle Eastern vibe of fruity acidic tastes in a savoury dish. If you don't have dates or dried apricots, use sultanas; if you can't find nibbed pistachios, use almonds; you can riff on my recipe. Enjoy with the tagine opposite and a heavy Middle Eastern wine, such as Sidi Brahim.

Spread the couscous onto a flat tray. Add the salt to the warm water and let it dissolve. Then, using your fingers, sprinkle the couscous with the water and rub it through your fingers, not letting it clump. Do this twice more, every 15 minutes. You will see that the grains have plumped up nicely without sticking together or getting waterlogged.

You will need a fine-mesh sieve, plus a saucepan with a tight-fitting lid. (Or use a couscoussière if you have one; I don't.) Put almost boiling water into the saucepan, deep enough so that it won't steam away, but not so deep that it touches the sieve. Add the ginger, coriander, cumin and chilli to the water.

Place the sieve over the pan and put your plumped-up couscous into the sieve with the dates or dried apricots. Wrap the lid in a clean tea towel and fit it onto the saucepan.

Place over a medium heat for 15–20 minutes to steam, checking the water level occasionally so that it doesn't boil dry.

When the couscous is cooked, tip into a bowl and mix in the coconut oil, pistachios, barberries, poppy seeds, cinnamon, rosewater, argan oil and bitter orange peel, if using. Garnish with the pomegranate seeds, if using.

Carrot, Pepper & Lentil Tagine

Serves 6

3 red peppers

5 tbsp olive oil

2 onions, sliced

3 garlic cloves, very
finely chopped

1 tsp ground cumin

½ tsp ground ginger

1 cinnamon stick

5 carrots, peeled and
thickly sliced

1 tbsp orange flower water

1 tbsp sultanas

200g red lentils

Pinch of saffron strands,
ground

500ml vegetable stock

Juice of ½ lemon

1 tbsp ras el hanout
spice mix

A dozen black olives,
stoned

A dozen dried apricots,
snipped into strips

Handful of sprigs of
flat-leaf parsley,
leaves picked

For the garnish:

Parsley and mint leaves
and/or dried rose
petals

Couple of preserved
lemons, sliced

Drizzle of argan oil

A tagine is both a method of cooking and a kind of Moroccan stewpot shaped like a cone. Condensation runs up the insides and back down into the food. If you don't have one, you can use a shallow casserole dish with a lid or, as many modern North Africans use, a pressure cooker.

Preheat the oven to 200°C/gas mark 6. Place the peppers on a baking tray and roast in the oven until the skin is puffy and blackened. Remove to a plastic food bag. Once cool enough to handle, strip the blackened skins from them, removing the seeds and stalks. Tear the peppers into strips. Reduce the oven temperature to 160°C/gas mark 2½ if using a casserole rather than a tagine or pressure cooker.

Place a tagine, flameproof casserole dish or pressure cooker over a medium heat. When hot, add the olive oil and then the onions and garlic. Sweat until softened, then add the remaining ingredients, one after the other, and stir well. If using a tagine, cover and cook for about 30 minutes (or follow the manufacturer's instructions and timings if using a pressure cooker). If using a casserole, cover and transfer to the oven to cook for 30—45 minutes.

Garnish with parsley and mint or dried rose petals, preserved lemons and a drizzle of argan oil, and serve with couscous (see opposite).

Freekeh with Purple Sprouting Broccoli & Almonds

Serves 4—6

200g freekeh (wholegrain)

500ml hot vegetable stock

70ml olive oil

1 onion, diced

2 garlic cloves, very finely chopped

1 cinnamon stick

1 tbsp sumac

50g blanched almonds

200g purple sprouting broccoli, trimmed

Sea salt

For the gremolata:

2 handfuls of curly parsley

1—2 garlic cloves, peeled

Grated zest of 1 lemon

Variation: Rather than frying the purple sprouting broccoli, make raw broccoli or cauliflower 'couscous' by processing it in a food processor. Let the freekeh cool slightly once cooked, then stir in 250g broccoli or cauliflower 'couscous'. Serves 8 as a big salad.

In my ongoing project to 'vary my grains' I picked up a box of the brilliantly named freekeh in my local ethnic shop.

Freekeh, when cooked, tastes nutty and new. But this green grain, fresh wheat from Arabia is as old as the hills and mentioned in the Bible. It's good for diabetes and contains more protein than rice or couscous. I fried it in olive oil and onions, then studded it with sprouting broccoli and almonds, and topped it with gremolata.

In a bowl, soak the freekeh in the hot stock for 10 minutes or so.

Heat the oil in a wide, shallow saucepan or deep-sided frying pan, add the onion and fry until soft, then add the garlic, cinnamon stick, sumac, almonds, purple sprouting broccoli and salt to taste. Cook until the broccoli is a little bit steamed, then add the soaked freekeh, stirring all the while.

Put the gremolata ingredients into a food processor (or use a hand-held blender) and blitz until finely chopped. Sprinkle it over the freekeh and serve.

Quinoa with Hazelnuts, Roasted Vegetables & Parsley

Serves 2—4

As I said opposite, I'm trying to eat different grains, not just pasta. Quinoa, pronounced 'keenwa' (I'm sure y'all knew that, but I feel I have to keep repeating it), has recently attracted controversy because some investigative journalists think that evil vegans are pricing out poor Peruvian farmers* from eating their own crop. How non-animal eaters could be entirely responsible for this, I'm not sure.

Supermarkets are now doing mixes of bulgur wheat and quinoa, which makes a change from the usual. Quinoa comes in several colours from white, pink, brown, black and red. The mix I used had red quinoa, which is nuttier and perhaps more flavoursome than the white more commonly found on grocery shelves. Quinoa isn't a grain but a grass that contains healthy fat and proteins, and it tricks the appetite into thinking you've had a nice bowl of starch.

Try this; it's not 'cheffy' but it is gorgeous tasting.

*I spent five months in Peru and Bolivia, mostly with Quechua-speaking villagers, and I didn't once have quinoa. We ate potatoes, rice and 'fideos' (macaroni). This was quite some time ago, in the early 90s, so maybe it wasn't popular then. It seems strange to claim that Andean dwellers now have a daily shortage of quinoa.

1 aubergine, halved lengthways and cut into strips

1 large red pepper, deseeded and finely sliced

6—10 baby carrots, tops trimmed, bottoms snipped

About 50ml olive oil

250g quinoa

75g hazelnuts

1 preserved lemon or lime, finely diced

Handful of basil leaves, rolled up together and finely sliced (this is a chiffonade)

Hazelnut oil, for drizzling

Sea salt

Preheat the oven to 200°C/gas mark 6.

Put the aubergine, pepper and carrots in a roasting tin, toss in enough olive oil to coat everything well and add 2 tsp salt. Roast for about 15 minutes until the aubergine and pepper are soft with slightly crispy edges.

Meanwhile, rinse the quinoa in a sieve until the water runs clear. Use double the volume of water to quinoa — in this case 500ml water — and put both in a medium saucepan with 1 tsp salt. Bring to the boil, then cook for about 20 minutes. Leave to stand for 5 minutes off the heat and with the lid on. Then uncover and fluff it up with a fork.

Toast the hazelnuts in a dry frying pan for 5 minutes. Mix the roasted vegetables, quinoa, hazelnuts, preserved lemon or lime and basil together, drizzle with hazelnut oil, season with salt to taste and serve.

Kasha & Bows

Serves 2–4

A Russian Jewish dish that I learnt from my friend Iris when I lived in Los Angeles for a while, way back when. A young photographer, doing freelance work for the *LA Weekly*, I also worked the graveyard shift in a top photo lab. Finishing at 4am, I'd go dancing to garage music and 'Tainted Love' in downtown clubs, then meet up with Iris at Canter's Deli, which was open 24/7. I even met a dowdy-looking Bette Midler in the queue, lining up with everyone else. Usually I'd order a root beer float and a bagel, but one night, Iris, a Russian Jewish girl from the valley, spotted a dish in the 'sides' section of the vast laminated menu. "Kasha and bows!" she exclaimed, "I was brought up on that." It was actually a very healthy and filling side dish that cost very little. Iris was one of the most beautiful girls I'd ever known: jet-black hair, pale blue, almond-shaped eyes and white skin. She spent a few years on heroin, which only made her pale eyes paler, for her pupils were tiny, and it made her skin even more alabaster in hue. she was like a punk Snow White.

I left the States after a couple of years — things got too murky. A girl was found dead in her apartment upstairs from mine. An escaped rapist broke into my flat, but I managed to act crazy and scare him off. There were rats living behind my wide retro American fridge. It was time to go home.

I'm happy to report that Iris Berry is now a renowned poet, and still beautiful. This is her aunt's recipe for kasha and bows.

Kasha is the Russian name for buckwheat, which comes in 2 types: roasted and unroasted. The roasted is darker and nuttier. You can buy this at Eastern European shops. It's not actually a grain; it's in the beetroot family and is therefore low GI and gluten free (although the bows are not).

100g roasted kasha buckwheat

200ml vegetable stock

250g dried farfalle pasta (bows)

50ml olive oil

2 large onions, roughly chopped

4 garlic cloves, very finely chopped

Juice of 1 lemon

Sea salt and freshly ground black pepper

Parsley leaves, to garnish

Get 2 medium saucepans. In one cook the kasha with the vegetable stock (this should take about 15 minutes) and in the other cook the pasta in boiling, salted water (12–15 minutes depending on the brand) until al dente.

Heat the oil in a large frying pan over a medium-high heat, then add the onions and cook until soft and caramelised. Add the garlic and cook until soft. Finally, add the kasha (which should have absorbed virtually all the stock during cooking) and the drained bows. Cook, tossing, until heated through and coated in the oil and onions. Squeeze the lemon juice over, add salt and pepper to taste, garnish with parsley leaves and serve.

Green Beans with Pink Soba Noodles, Miso, Pecans, Pink Pickled Ginger & Purple Umeboshi Plums

Serves 4

I had something like this at a fantastic Japanese restaurant in Soho called Koya. Pink soba noodles are flavoured with plums and you can also buy them in green (green tea-flavoured), black or white. They cook very quickly and have no gluten (though you should check the label, as some soba noodles contain wheat). In this recipe, you eat them cold — sounds weird, huh? Actually it works: the hot beans, cold noodles, salty fudgy taste of nuts and miso, and vinegary heat of ginger.

Soba noodles are the healthiest fast food, ready in minutes. If you are a bit dubious about the cold noodle thing, or unable to get hold of soba noodles, you could of course use any soft noodles for this, like rice or wheat (udon) noodles, which you can often buy ready-cooked, just necessitating a bit of heating up.

The pickled ginger can be bought in Asian shops or online. Here I'm talking about the dark pink shredded stuff rather than the salmon-pink slivers we find in sushi bars.

(Photo on page 114.)

200g green beans (you can also use 'wax beans', which are a paler colour, or any combo of long beans)

3cm piece of fresh ginger, peeled and chopped

2 tbsp miso

80g pecan nuts

2 tsp soy sauce, or to taste

2 tbsp rice wine vinegar

1 tbsp mirin

1 tbsp sesame oil

200g pink soba noodles (check the label to make sure they are vegan)

4 tbsp shredded dark pink pickled ginger

8 purple umeboshi plums

Sea salt

Bring a saucepan of water to the boil and add salt. Cook the beans for about 5 minutes until bright green and just tender. Drain and plunge into cold water, then drain again. Set aside in a bowl.

Put the fresh ginger, miso, pecans, soy sauce, rice wine vinegar, mirin and sesame oil in a food processor and grind together.

Then bring another medium saucepan of salted water to the boil and plunge in the pink soba noodles. They will cook quickly, — in about 5 minutes. Drain and rinse in cold water.

Toss the beans in the ginger pecan sauce and plate the noodles, piling the beans on top. Serve with dark pink pickled ginger and 2 umeboshi plums per person.

Fresh Vegan Pasta

Makes approximately 400g fresh pasta, serves 2—4

This is more or less the same recipe as normal fresh pasta but obviously without the egg. If you want yellow egg-like pasta, just add a little ground turmeric to the dough. It's important to get hard wheat (grano duro) pasta flour (00) because it will add gluten and stretchiness, which you need because you don't have the egg. You can make pasta with just oil and water, but I did find that the egg replacer introduced smoothness and stretchiness to the pasta dough.

If you can't get hold of 00 pasta flour, then use three parts strong white bread flour to one part plain flour (i.e.: for 250g use (rounding up) 190g strong white bread flour to 60g plain flour).

250g Italian 00 pasta flour

1 tsp sea salt

75ml water

3 tbsp olive oil OR 90ml water mixed with 1 tsp egg replacer

Fine semolina, for dusting

If mixing by hand, put the flour and salt into a bowl, make a well in the middle and add the water, and the oil or water and egg replacer. Stir with a wooden spoon, then knead it together with your hands. Good pasta is all about texture; it mustn't be too dry or too wet. Form a ball, cover with clingfilm and leave to rest at room temperature for 30 minutes. The resting time is important, as this will make the dough more flexible.

If using a food processor, put the flour and salt in and slowly pulse in the water, and the oil or water and egg replacer. Stop when it looks like large couscous. Then remove the dough, form a ball and knead it by hand for several minutes until well combined. Continue as for by hand.

Once the dough has rested, divide in half. Use one half at a time, leaving the other half covered with clingfilm or a damp clean tea towel as you work. If you have a pasta maker, run the ball through it on the widest setting. Then fold the dough over and run it through the machine several times, folding over each time and inserting the open end into the machine. Eventually you will see a bubble form and/or a popping sound as the folded end goes into the pasta machine. This means the pasta is ready to roll.

Thread the flattened oval of pasta through the machine (no longer folding it over) on each setting, starting at the widest and narrowing it by one notch each time. By

notch 5 you will probably have to cut your tongue
of pasta in half, unless you have an assistant or
unbelievably long arms. Continue to run the pasta
through the machine and stop before the last notch
(usually 7) because you don't want the dough so
thin that it will break and leak the contents while
cooking. Hang up the pasta tongues to dry (I use my
wooden washing line(!) but you can buy wooden pasta
dryers) for 10—15 minutes or so. However you don't
want it to dry too much or it will break.

If you don't have a machine, then roll the pasta out
very thinly on a floured surface, making quarter turns
as in pastry, until it is about 2mm thick.

Then change the flat pasta roller on the machine for
the shape of pasta you want to cut, or if you are
making it without a machine, roll up the oval of dough
loosely and make perpendicular cuts all along, every
5mm, so that you end up with coils of flat, thin pasta.

For ravioli, you can cut circles with a small glass,
add the filling to one and press a second circle on
top, brushing the edges with water and pinching them
together (you can also buy several types of ravioli
cutter in kitchen shops).

The second problem with pasta, once you have made it,
is to stop it sticking. I sprinkle a thick layer of
fine semolina on a tray and spread the pasta out on
top. In fact, while I'm making long pasta shapes in
the machine, I hold the tray underneath so that the
pasta falls straight into the semolina flour. With
finer pasta such as fettuccine, curl it into nests,
liberally sprinkling with the semolina, and leave to
air-dry for a day. If I'm not using it straightaway,
I freeze it on the tray (so choose a tray that fits
into your freezer shelves). Once it is frozen, you can
tip it into a plastic freezer bag and store it for up
to 3 months. Remember NEVER wash your pasta machine,
or it will go rusty. Clean it with a dry brush.

To cook the pasta, always add salt to a large saucepan
of water and bring to the boil. Cook the pasta for
1—5 minutes until it floats to the surface. Ravioli can
take a bit longer — 5—10 minutes — but don't walk away
from the stove!

Flower & Herb Pasta

Serves 4

I make edible geranium, dill, sage and nasturtium noodles by adding these just before I start rolling the pasta. The flowers stretch, but it looks so pretty, like floral lisle stockings! Roll up loosely and cut wide noodles. Cook very quickly (3–5 minutes) in boiling, salted water and serve with olive oil, chopped fresh herbs, more flowers, pine nuts and black pepper.

Kale Pesto

100g kale or cavolo nero

75g pine nuts

2 tbsp nutritional yeast

3 garlic cloves, peeled

100ml olive oil

50ml sunflower oil

2 tbsp lemon juice

Sea salt

Cut the thick stems from the kale or cavolo nero and pull off the rest of the leaves.

Put the pine nuts, nutritional yeast, garlic and kale into a food processor and whizz until finely chopped.

With the motor still running, drizzle in the oils and lemon juice. Add salt to taste.

Vegan Pesto Alla Genovese

This recipe from Genoa is traditionally made with basil and pine nuts, but there is also a *pesto alla trapanese*, from Trapani in Sicily, made with walnuts or almonds in place of the pine nuts.

Large bunch of basil, leaves only

1 garlic clove, peeled

50g pine nuts

50ml olive oil

2 tbsp nutritional yeast

Juice of ½ lemon

Sea salt

Pulse all the ingredients in a food processor until they form a paste. Add salt to taste.

Watercress & Lemon Zest Pesto

100g watercress

Grated zest of 1 lemon

2 tbsp pine nuts

3 tbsp nut or olive oil

Freshly ground black pepper

Whizz the ingredients together in a food processor until combined. Add pepper to taste.

Chocolate Sichuan Pepper Fettuccine with Porcini & Black Olives

Serves 4

For the chocolate fettuccine:

250g Italian 00 pasta flour

1 tsp sea salt, plus extra for cooking the pasta

1 tsp very finely ground Sichuan or other pepper

50g cocoa powder

115ml water

165ml water mixed with 1 tsp egg replacer

Fine semolina, for dusting

For the sauce:

20g dried porcini

100ml boiling water

50ml olive oil

3 shallots, thinly sliced

2 garlic cloves, very finely chopped

1 tsp sea salt

100g fresh ceps or other wild or brown mushrooms, thinly sliced

A dozen stoned black olives

Juice of ½ lemon

100ml soya cream

To serve:

Basil leaves

Freshly ground black pepper

Make the fettuccine following the instructions on page 122, and adding the pepper and cocoa powder at the same time as the flour and salt.

Cover the dried porcini with the boiling water and leave to soak for at least 30 minutes. Drain and reserve the soaking water.

Meanwhile, heat the oil in a medium frying pan over a medium heat, sweat the shallots, adding the garlic and salt, then add the fresh mushrooms and the olives. As the sauce reduces, gradually add the porcini soaking liquid until it develops a thickened but pouring consistency. Add the lemon juice and leave to rest, then add the soya cream just before serving. (The sauce develops flavour if left a while.)

Fill a large saucepan with water and bring to the boil with at least 1 tbsp sea salt.

Making sure the fettuccine is in separate strands before you put it in the water, drop it in the boiling water and be ready to scoop it out when it floats. Depending on how thick your pasta is, this can take only a minute.

Place the pasta in the middle of the dish and drape the sauce over it.

Benign Dictatorship Saffron Spaghetti

Serves 6 with leftover sauce

This is my Death Row dish. I could pretty much eat this every day. Spaghetti Napoli or Napolitana — or spaghetti with tomato sauce — is simple and beautiful, a mainstay of my family life. Does it come from Naples? Yeah, probs. Southern Italy was, is, poorer and hotter than the north and so, not only were they growing ace tomatoes but they could also not afford to add meat to their pasta sauce. Who needs meat when great tomatoes provide all the umami oomph you could possibly want? So 'Bolognese' from Bologna (in northern Italy), the classic mincemeat and tomato spaghetti sauce, became 'Napolitana' (from the south), an infinitely chic-er dish.

Another reason for the popularity of the meatless sauce is that tomatoes used to be more acidic until it was bred out of them. A Napoli sauce was something you could preserve, conveniently bottled on long journeys, for the winter.

It's strange to think about the process of 'nation branding' and how misleading it can be. I recently attended a talk where it was explained that the great English breakfast was only about 150 years old, invented, like so much else including Christmas, in the Victorian times. When we think about Italy and its 'USP', we visualise the red, white and green of the flag. The red is the tomato, the white is the pasta and the green is the basil.

But the tomato is fairly new to Italy, arriving after the discovery of America, via Spain in the 16th century. Furthermore, pasta was reserved for feast days, only becoming regularly available to the poor when the manufacturing process was mechanised in the late 19th century.

Spaghetti Napoli was the second recipe I was ever taught by my mother. I'd decided, at a ridiculously early age, to host a dinner party for 15 people, with 3 courses. The dinner party was a bit of a disaster: starters went out at 11pm, I got far too drunk and my best friend got off with the boy that this whole shenanigans was constructed for. But I learnt how to make this dish, so it wasn't a write-off.

5 tbsp olive oil, plus a large glug

2 onions, diced

4–5 garlic cloves, finely chopped

5 bay leaves, ideally fresh

3–4 x 400g tins or jars of tomatoes, or 1kg fresh tomatoes

Large pinch of saffron strands

1 sprig of oregano (optional)

700g good-quality dried spaghetti (I generally work on 100g cooked per person for a starter, 150g cooked for a main)

Sea salt and plenty of freshly ground black pepper

This sauce is really simple if you follow my instructions exactly. Do not freestyle it, something I generally give you permission to do in other recipes. No, this is a benign dictatorship when it comes to spaghetti.

Before we start, a few rules:

1. On no account add sugar. The French add sugar, which is why they are terrible at pasta even if they are good at everything else. If you want a sweeter sauce, wait a day before eating it. It will become sweeter.

2. Buy the best tomatoes you can afford — fresh or tinned. If you are buying tinned tomatoes, DO NOT buy those watery cheap tins containing 3 flayed plum-shaped tomatoes and a load of thin red juice. Buy the most expensive. Hell, go crazy, save yourself some effort and buy ready-chopped.

Organic is good. I used Così Com'è bottled tomatoes (yellow and red) in this recipe, and their flavour is extraordinary. I don't care how poor you are, I don't care if you have had all your savings seized; you can buy a halfway-decent tin of tomatoes.

3. Buy the best spaghetti you can afford. NOT quick-cook. The longer the cooking time on the packet, the better. Buy 11-minute spaghetti, bronze-die preferably (this gives the surface a roughness that means the sauce adheres). If you buy very good pasta, it's almost impossible to overcook it. Brands I recommend: Barilla, De Cecco, Garofalo.

4. Salt your pasta water. Salt it until it is as salty as the Mediterranean Sea. With sea salt. If you have sufficiently seasoned your water, you will not need to add salt at the table. Geddit?

Heat the oil in a large pan, add the onions and cook until soft. Add the garlic and bay leaves. Stir. Add the tomatoes. I tend to squeeze the tomatoes, tearing them as I go, into the pan (fresh tomatoes I will chop up). Stir in 1 tbsp salt, the saffron and oregano, if using (if you have fresh, but don't bother with out-of-date dried oregano. In fact, go through your spice cupboard, check the dates and chuck most of it out. In India, housewives buy small quantities of fresh spices WEEKLY. This is what we should be doing).

Simmer, uncovered, for 45 minutes over a low heat, if you have time. It's pretty good after 20 minutes. If I'm drinking red wine, I might sling in half a glass if the sauce is getting too concentrated.

The pasta bit:

Get a large or tall saucepan. Don't use a small saucepan. Really. It's the same as salads. Why do people try to squash a salad into a tiny bowl? You can't toss the salad in the dressing! So if you haven't got a big pasta saucepan, it's time you invested in one. It's about £30 for something you'll probably use every day for the next decade.

Get a big load of salty boiling water on the go. Boil 3 or 4 kettles if necessary and fill it up that way. Throw in a handful of sea salt. Yes: a handful. It's fine, don't worry. Feel the fear and do it anyway.

When it's bubbling, put the spaghetti in, pushing down gradually until it's all submerged. Stir a couple of times during cooking to keep the strands separate. Cook for a minute less than they say on the packet and have your colander ready in the sink.

Strain out the pasta quickly, then dump it back into the hot saucepan. Splash a large glug of olive oil over the hot pasta, stirring it, to prevent the pasta sticking together.

If you are being mamma at the table, have a stack of bowls, put the lid on the pasta and take both the pasta and the sauce to the table. Serve into each bowl at the table, pasta first, sauce on top. Yes I know Jamie Oliver says add the pasta to the sauce, but it looks prettier this way and people like different amounts of sauce. Make sure there is a pepper mill at the table.

Beetroot Pelmeni with Herb & Walnut Filling

Makes 80—90 pelmeni, serves 6—8

If you live near any Eastern European shops, buy a pelmeni mould (otherwise use a ravioli cutter or a pasta machine that has a ravioli cutter). This is a fusion of Polish pelmeni and a Georgian walnut stuffing.

300g cooked beetroot (or 3 tsp beetroot powder mixed with 1 tbsp water)

1 tsp sea salt

500g Italian 00 pasta flour

5 tbsp olive oil

5 tbsp warm water mixed with 1 tbsp egg replacer

Extra pasta flour or fine semolina, for dusting

For the filling:

300g walnuts

½ tsp coriander seeds

1 tsp ground marigold petals (organic, unsprayed)

1 tsp sea salt

2 garlic cloves, very finely chopped

Handful of coriander leaves

Pinch of fenugreek seeds

1 tbsp red wine vinegar

Small handfuls of mixed herbs, such as parsley, coriander, pennyroyal, dill and tarragon

To serve:

A little walnut oil

Pomegranate seeds

Marigold petals

Put the cooked beetroot, if using, in a food processor and pulse to a purée. Add the salt.

Put the flour into a large bowl and make a well in the middle. Tip in the beetroot purée and mix to a dough, then gradually add the olive oil followed by the beetroot powder paste, if using, and the water and egg replacer, checking all the time to make sure you have just the right consistency for the pasta. (If using a food processor, add the hot water a tablespoon at a time with the machine running until the pasta forms large grains. Then knead together by hand.) Shape into a ball, cover with clingfilm and leave it to rest at room temperature.

In a powerful food processor, finely grind the walnuts. Tip out and put the coriander seeds, marigold petals, salt, garlic, coriander leaves and fenugreek in the processor. Whizz to a paste, then mix this with the walnuts, vinegar and mixed chopped herbs. (This paste, with added oil, also makes a good pesto.)

Divide the rested dough into 4 pieces, and work with one at a time, keeping the other pieces covered in clingfilm so that they don't dry out. Roll out the dark pink dough as thinly as you can (or use a pasta machine — see the pasta recipe on page 122) to a circle slightly bigger than the pelmeni mould. Lay one sheet over the mould, then spoon ½ tsp filling mixture into each compartment. Lay another sheet of pasta on top, sealing with water and pressing firmly around the sides.

Transfer the pelmeni to a large baking sheet dusted with flour or semolina, making sure they are in a single layer. You can freeze them like this, then once frozen, they can be dumped into a plastic bag in the freezer.

Fill a large saucepan with boiling, salted water. Drop the fresh pelmeni into the boiling water and cook until they start to float. Make sure they don't overcook. Drain and serve with walnut oil, pomegranate seeds and marigold petals.

Steamed Gyoza with Mushroom & Tofu Filling

Makes 24

This is basically an Asian version of ravioli or, to be historically accurate, the other way around, for pasta came from China. Buy the little circles of 'pasta' from Chinese or Japanese shops, but check carefully that they don't contain egg. I made these gyoza in a wok that fitted my bamboo steamer just perfectly. A bamboo steamer is very cheap, or you can use a metal steamer. You need a flat surface, as you don't want to have the gyoza touching each other; they will stick and rip the skin off.

3 tbsp sesame oil

2 garlic cloves,
    very finely chopped

Thumb of ginger,
    peeled and very
    finely chopped

1 tbsp sugar

3 tbsp dark soy
    sauce

1 tsp Chinese
    five-spice

1 tsp cornflour

200g firm tofu

4 spring onions,
    sliced, white and
    green parts set
    aside separately

250g shiitake or
    other mushrooms,
    finely sliced

1 packet of 24 gyoza
    or Chinese wonton
    skins

Rice flour or plain
    white flour, for
    dusting

Plum sauce, to serve

Variation:
Add finely chopped
Baechu Kimchi
(see page 23) to
the filling.

To make the filling, put the sesame oil, garlic, ginger, sugar, soy sauce, five-spice and cornflour into a hot wok or frying pan and sizzle for a couple of minutes. Drain and dice the tofu, then add to the wok or pan and fry for 5 minutes. Add the white slices of spring onions and the mushrooms and fry for 3—5 minutes (they will release a lot of liquid).

Place a sieve over a bowl. Tip all the mixture into the sieve and let the excess liquid drain out (you don't want a very liquid filling, as the gyoza skins will not hold it).

Then set up a little gyoza filling station on a table: a small bowl of water, a stack of gyoza skins, the cooled filling and a teaspoon. Lay out a gyoza skin, dip your finger into the water and run it around the border of the gyoza skin. Put a heaped teaspoon of filling into the middle, then bring up the sides and press them together to seal the gyoza like crescent-shaped dumplings.

Set aside each dumpling on a tray sprinkled generously with flour so that they won't stick to the bottom when you remove them to steam. When you have shaped them all, place in a steamer, spaced slightly apart. Take a piece of greaseproof paper and cut into the shape of your steamer. Run it under the tap to moisten it.

Prepare a large pot or wok of boiling water and place the steamer over it. Put the circle of moist greaseproof paper over the gyoza, then put on the lid. Steam for about 20 minutes, depending on how fresh they are, and on the thickness of the skins. They are cooked when they are translucent. Then fry in a pan too, if you like. Serve with the reserved green spring onion slices and the plum sauce for dipping.

Three-Topping Polenta Party

Serves 5

2.25 litres water
  (for quick-cook
  polenta use only
  1.5 litres)

1 tbsp sea salt

500g fine polenta

50ml olive oil

Three toppings:

Peperonata (below)

Artichokes in oil

Grilled fennel
  slices

Variations:
Pesto (page 124),
caramelised onions
with garlic,
mushrooms in cashew
cream and garlic,
Napolitana sauce
(page 126), grilled
aubergines, braised
endives, leeks,
cardoons

I made this at my vegan supper club with big-time vegan cookery author, Terry Hope Romero. Tickets sold out within a day. Interestingly, on the night, half our guests weren't vegan but vegan-curious meat eaters.

Boil the water in a large, good-quality, heavy-bottomed saucepan (you don't want a thin bottom on your cookware anyway). Add the salt and then the polenta. Keep stirring. With the slow-cook polenta, it can take 90 minutes. The quick-cook takes about 2 minutes. What's the difference? The slow-cook is a little more 'corny', a little grittier and possibly better for a dinner party in that it stays soft for longer. You want a nice, thick soupy polenta that you can spoon onto a wooden board; not too thick but not so thin that it runs off the board.

Spoon the polenta onto the board and spread it out. Drizzle with the olive oil and add the warmed toppings in stripes on top. Serve by giving everyone a spoon to help themselves. Fun and interactive!

Got leftover polenta? Cut into slices and grill. Serve for breakfast with diced jalapeños, tomatoes, onion and coriander salsa with plenty of lime juice.

Peperonata

Serves 2—4

About 100ml olive oil

7 Romano peppers

1 yellow pepper

1 onion, sliced

3 garlic cloves, finely chopped

1 tsp sweet smoked paprika

1 tbsp each chopped
  marjoram and oregano

2 bay leaves

Glug of verjuice

2 tbsp drained capers

1 tbsp drained pickled green
  peppercorns (optional)

Sea salt

Preheat the oven to 180°C/gas mark 4. Oil a baking tray with some of the oil. Put all the peppers on it whole, toss in more oil and roast for 15—20 minutes. Take them out, strip off the skins, remove the stalks and seeds and cut the flesh into 2cm strips. Pour any tasty oil from the tray into a heavy, ovenproof pan with a lid and add more olive oil. Add the onion and sweat, without letting it burn; it should be soft. Add the garlic, paprika, 1 tbsp salt, the herbs and verjuice.

Add the pepper strips. Put the lid on and cook in the oven for 45 minutes. The peppers should be soft and sweet. Add the capers and peppercorns, if using, check the seasoning and serve warm or cold.

Uthappam

Makes 8 uthappam

Uthappam is frequently referred to as a kind of Indian pizza, but having made it, it was more like large, shallow sub-continental crumpet. It's one of the best things I have made in ages. I chose to top it with onions fried in oil with mustard seeds and curry leaves.

First you must make the batter, which is a lengthy process but it is important to make sure that it ferments to the right flavour and texture. You'll need to start prepping several days in advance of serving.

For the dhosa batter:

275g broken or par-boiled rice (available in Indian shops under these names)

½ tsp fenugreek seeds

65g urad dhal (white lentils), skinless and preferably whole

300ml water

1 tsp sugar

1 tbsp sea salt

Vegetable oil, for frying

For the topping, per uthappam:

2 tbsp vegetable or coconut oil

½ tsp cumin seeds

½ tsp mustard seeds

1 small onion, red or yellow, finely sliced into rings

1 green chilli, thinly sliced

Large pinch of curry leaves, fresh or dried

Pinch of sea salt

For the dhosa batter, soak the rice and fenugreek in plenty of cold water for 12 hours. Thirty minutes before the end of the soaking, put the urad dhal separately in plenty of water to soak.

Drain the rice and dhal and grind really well together in a blender or food processor with the fresh water, in 2 batches (I use a Vitamix, which grinds very finely), until frothy, smooth and chalky.

Put the batter in a bowl and cover with a tea towel. Leave to ferment at room temperature (not in the fridge, unless you live in a hot country like India) for 3—4 days, checking every day. When it's bubbly and tastes a bit sour, it's fermented. This is very important because if you cook the batter when it isn't sufficiently fermented, the uthappam will be heavy and tasteless. Stir in the sugar and salt.

For the topping, heat the oil in a small frying pan. Add the cumin seeds, then the mustard seeds. Let them pop. Then add the onion, chilli and curry leaves and cook until the edges of the onion are golden and the centres are soft.

Heat a little oil in a tava or flat pancake pan, then put in half a ladle of the dhosa batter. The batter circle should be about 8—10cm in diameter and 5mm thick. Let the bottom cook (it will form air bubbles, like a crumpet), then spoon the onion mixture on top. Sprinkle over a pinch of salt and eat it all up. Then, probably, make another one and eat that all up too. Mmmm.

Pizzette with Roast Pumpkin, Red Onion & Sage

Makes 2

For the dough:

250g strong white bread flour

1 tsp sea salt

1 tsp fast-action dried yeast

1 tsp caster sugar

200ml lukewarm water

1 tbsp olive oil, plus extra for oiling

Fine semolina, for dusting

For the topping:

500g pumpkin, deseeded and sliced into crescents

1½ tsp sea salt

4 tbsp olive oil, plus extra for drizzling

1 red onion, sliced

2 garlic cloves, finely chopped

Handful of sage leaves

Grated zest of 1 lemon (optional)

I made these for an *Eat, Pray, Love* supper club, commissioned by the film distributors. The film's protagonist, played by Julia Roberts, was depressed even though she had a) a lovely husband b) a gorgeous lover c) a great job as a successful writer. She recovered by going to Italy and eating great pizza. In the film. I'm not sure Julia Roberts ever eats pizza irl. These pizzette have a seasonal, autumnally inspired topping. It's a great recipe for Halloween or a bonfire party.

Preheat the oven to 200°C/gas mark 6. Place a large baking sheet in to heat up.

Put the flour and salt into a large bowl. Mix the yeast, sugar and water in a jug and leave to bubble for about 5 minutes. Pour the yeast mixture into the flour and add the olive oil.

Mix together, then knead the dough on the work surface until smooth. (You can use a food processor up to this stage, if you prefer.) Put back in the bowl, cover and leave to rest in a warm place for 1 hour.

In the meantime, toss the pumpkin slices and salt in the olive oil on a lipped baking tray. (You can peel the pumpkin slices, but I don't bother. The skin is quite thin and not unpleasant.) Roast for 15—20 minutes or until soft and caramelised around the edges, then add the red onion and garlic and roast for another 10 minutes.

Tip the risen dough out onto an oiled surface, cut into 2 pieces and roll each piece into a circle. It doesn't matter if the circles aren't perfect — that's all part of the homemade look!

Then dust 2 pieces of baking parchment with semolina and place a dough circle on each. Arrange the pumpkin and onion over the pizzette, scatter sage leaves all over and drizzle with olive oil.

Slide both pizzette, on their baking parchment, onto the hot baking sheet in the oven and bake for 10—12 minutes. Remove from the oven and sprinkle over the lemon zest, if using. Serve with a simple watercress salad.

Hibiscus Flowers in Blue Corn Enchiladas with Pickled Purple Cabbage

Serves 7 (2 enchiladas each)

For the filling:

100g dried hibiscus flowers
  (or fresh if you have access
  to a plant)

50ml olive oil

1 large onion, thinly sliced

3 garlic cloves, minced

2 large carrots, grated

100g daikon radish, grated

50g sugar

½ tsp dried oregano

¼ tsp dried thyme

Sea salt and freshly ground
  black pepper

For the pickled purple cabbage:

100g sugar

20g sea salt

200ml red wine vinegar

¼ red cabbage, very thinly sliced

For the chipotle tomato sauce:

2 tbsp vegetable oil

1 white onion, sliced

3 fresh bay leaves

1 tbsp fresh or dried oregano

1 tbsp fresh or dried thyme

3 garlic cloves, thinly sliced

1kg ripe plum tomatoes, quartered

5 tbsp purple cabbage pickle
  juice, or to taste (see above)

2 dried chipotles, deseeded,
  plus 1 tbsp pickled jalapeños
  or 2 chipotles in adobo sauce

350 ml water

For the tofu sour cream:

400g silken tofu, drained

1 tbsp olive oil

Juice of 1 lemon

½ tsp sea salt

For the tortillas and to assemble:

Vegetable oil, for oiling and frying

14 x 15cm-diameter blue (or white)
  corn tortillas

Vegan cheese, such as No-Moo Melty
  cheese from Vegusto, sliced

I had something similar to this cooked by a woman chef Pilar Cabrera from Oaxaca at Azul Condesa restaurant in Mexico City, or DF ('Dey Effe') as the locals call it. While it's a typical Oaxacan dish, it is very unusual, with a tangy flavour. The red hibiscus with the blue corn enchiladas and the pickled purple cabbage lend this dish deep sunset colours. And blue corn is the only truly blue food! It's easy to buy hibiscus flowers online and at health-food shops.

The more unusual ingredients are readily available on Mexican food websites. I urge you to discover chipotle in adobo — just one of which can transform a sauce, a stew or a vegan mayonnaise dish.

To make the filling, place the hibiscus flowers in a heatproof bowl, cover with boiling water and leave to steep overnight. (At the same time, prepare your purple pickled cabbage to leave overnight.)

In the morning, strain the flowers. Heat the olive oil in a large, heavy pan over a medium heat, add the onion and garlic and sauté until soft. Add the hibiscus flowers, carrots, daikon, sugar, oregano and thyme. Cook, stirring, for about 15 minutes until the carrots are soft and the liquid has evaporated. Season with salt and pepper and set aside to keep warm.

For the pickled purple cabbage, put the sugar, salt and vinegar in a small saucepan and simmer until dissolved. Let it cool, then toss with the cabbage in a bowl and leave to stand overnight. The next day, drain the cabbage, reserving the liquid.

For the chipotle tomato sauce, heat the vegetable oil in a saucepan and fry the onion until soft, then add the bay leaves, oregano, thyme, garlic, tomatoes, some salt, the pickle juice, chipotles and water. Place over a medium heat and cook, stirring occasionally, for about 20 minutes until the tomatoes begin to fall apart. Remove from the heat and remove the bay leaves. Transfer the mixture to a blender and purée until smooth.

To make the tofu sour cream, whisk the ingredients together and store in the fridge until ready to use.

Oil a large roasting tin and preheat the oven to 180°C/gas mark 4. Pour enough of the tomato sauce to cover the bottom of the roasting tin.

Pour enough oil into a large frying pan to reach a depth of 2cm. Heat over medium-high heat. Working in batches, submerge the tortillas and cook, turning once, for 30–45 seconds until they soften. Drain on kitchen paper. (A lower-fat option is to steam the tortillas in a vegetable steamer, or microwave them in a tortilla warmer.)

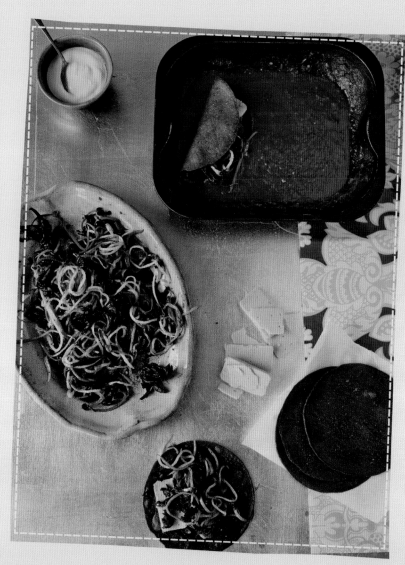

To assemble, put a small amount of hibiscus filling in the centre of each tortilla, plus a slice of the cheese, then roll to enclose, placing them all in the roasting tin on top of the sauce. Smother the enchiladas with more tomato sauce and bake in the oven for 10 minutes. Garnish with the tofu sour cream and pickled purple cabbage, and serve.

Smoked, Basil & Beetroot Tofu Baked in Coconut

Serves 4–6

1 pack of banana leaves, cut into 30cm squares (1 per guest)

200g basil tofu, drained and cut into 5mm slices (to make your own, see page 33)

200g smoked tofu, drained and cut into 5mm slices

200g firm tofu, dyed with 1 tbsp beetroot powder rubbed in or plain, cut into 5mm slices

4–6 small bird's eye chillies, deseeded and thinly sliced

Thumb of ginger, peeled and very finely chopped

250ml coconut cream

Tamari sauce, for drizzling

Handful of coriander leaves

I do like to cook things 'en papillote' — that is, wrapped in leaves or baking parchment — as it seals in all the flavour. I specify cooking this in banana leaves, but you can use baking parchment if you like. This is a real dinner party dish. Banana leaves are cheapest if bought frozen in Asian/Chinese supermarkets.

Preheat the oven to 200°C/gas mark 6.

First prepare the banana leaves by roasting them slightly over an open flame or dry-roasting them in a large frying pan, until they soften. Don't let them burn or go black. Then lay the banana squares flat and arrange the different coloured slices of tofu, overlapping one another, on top.

Add a few slices of chilli, a pinch of chopped ginger, 1 tbsp coconut cream, a drizzle of tamari sauce and a few coriander leaves to each. Close the packages, using either kitchen string or cocktail sticks. Place them carefully in a baking tray and bake for 25 minutes.

Serve with noodles or rice and a citrus salad (see page 99).

Stuffed Yellow Courgettes & Red Peppers

Serves 4—6

1 whole garlic bulb

Olive oil, for roasting and frying

100g unroasted kasha buckwheat

200ml vegetable stock

5 small, round yellow courgettes

3 small Romano peppers

200g cauliflower florets

200g broccoli florets

4 cherry tomatoes, quartered

Couple of sprigs of thyme, leaves only

Sea salt and freshly ground black pepper

Preheat the oven to 200°C/gas mark 6. Toss the garlic bulb in olive oil and roast on a baking tray for about 15 minutes or until softened. Then remove from the oven, let cool and squeeze out the softened middles of the cloves. Set aside. (You can do more of these and keep them in a little bowl in the fridge, useful for many recipes.)

Put the kasha and stock in a pan, cover and bring to the boil. Turn down to a simmer and cook until all the water is absorbed, as when cooking rice.

When I cook, I often start with colour. In my mind's eye, I saw a yellow and red dish with a little bit of green, and I had some round sunflower-yellow courgettes and postbox-red Romano peppers in the fridge. Slice off the top of the courgettes, retaining the 'hat', then hollow out the centres, making sure you don't gouge any holes in the side. Cut the stalk ends off the peppers, deseed and cut each into 3 rings. Pack the courgettes and peppers into an oiled, medium-sized baking dish, alternating the colours.

Then, do this new thing that's all the rage: make couscous from vegetables. You just put the raw cauliflower and broccoli florets into a food processor and process until they look like couscous. (You can also use this technique to make a raw salad.)

Mix the kasha and vegetable couscous with the cherry tomatoes. Heat some olive oil in a frying pan, add this mixture along with the roast garlic cloves and thyme leaves and fry for about 5 minutes, then add salt and pepper to taste.

Spoon the mixture into the courgettes and peppers, making sure you can see a little bit of red cherry tomato in the yellow courgette stuffing. If there is any tasty oil left from the garlic clove roasting and the couscous frying, drizzle that over the courgettes and peppers. Replace the 'hats' on all of them.

Cover the dish with foil and bake in the oven (still at 200°C/gas mark 6) for 15—20 minutes, removing the foil for the last 5 minutes.

Chocolate Smoky Tofu Mole in Tacos with Grilled Calçots

Serves 4—8

In Oaxaca, they have all kinds of *mole*, a kind of paste or thick sauce — yellow, green, red — but a chocolate *mole* is one of the most unique. This chocolate *mole* with smoked tofu is as satisfying as any meat dish. Calçots are a Catalan dish of very young leeks simply grilled, slightly blackened and dressed with olive oil. A great combo for tacos. The typically Oaxacan sauce will make double the amount you need for the tofu, so either freeze half or, if you have more guests, double the amount of tofu. You can serve this as tacos or just as a stew with rice.

2½ tbsp olive oil

1 onion, diced

3 garlic cloves, very finely chopped

60g vegan dark chocolate

350g tomatoes, left whole

1 tsp ground cumin

½ tsp ground cinnamon

¼ tsp ground allspice

2 dried ancho chillies

2 dried chipotle chillies

2 tbsp vegetable stock powder

170g blanched or ground almonds

2 tbsp strong agave nectar

400g firm smoked tofu, drained and cut into 2.5cm cubes

1 pack of calçots, young leeks or spring onions, trimmed

14 corn tortillas

Sea salt

To serve:

Slices of avocado

A fistful of alfalfa sprouts

Sprigs of coriander

Lime wedges

Heat the oil in a pan and fry the onion and garlic until soft, then add the chocolate, tomatoes, cumin, cinnamon and allspice. Cook slowly over a low-medium heat for 15—20 minutes while you prepare the chillies.

Meanwhile, split all the dried chillies and empty out the seeds, then briefly toast the chillies in a dry frying pan until soft. Place in a ½-litre heatproof jug with the vegetable stock powder. Fill up the jug with boiling water and leave to soak for 10 minutes, stirring once or twice.

Put the almonds, the chilli and stock mixture, the cooked sauce, agave nectar and 1 tbsp salt in a powerful blender. Starting on a low speed, process together, increasing the speed as you go, until smooth. Transfer the sauce to a deep, wide frying pan.

Add the tofu cubes to the sauce and poach until the tofu expands slightly and the sauce is bubbling but not boiling.

In the meantime, roast the calçots, young leeks or spring onions in a dry frying pan or directly over a flame, turning them, until soft and slightly blackened around the edges (this makes them sweet).

To serve, place some of the tofu pieces and the chocolate mole in the tacos and fold so that the opening is upwards. Tuck in a leek or spring onion and a few avocado slices. Top with alfalfa sprouts, the calçots and coriander. Season with salt and squeeze over some lime juice.

142

Ital Stew with Ginger Cristophenes & Trinidadian Green Seasoning

Serves 6

3 tbsp coconut oil

4 spring onions, chopped into 5cm lengths

3 garlic cloves, very finely chopped

10 pimento (allspice) berries

3 carrots, peeled and finely sliced into rounds

1 ripe plantain, peeled and cut into 2cm slices

400g tin of black-eyed beans, drained

400ml tin of coconut milk

500ml vegetable stock

540g tin of callaloo

2 large yams (purple or yellow) or eddoes, peeled and cut into quarters or eighths (or 1kg pumpkin, cut into thick slices)

2 sweet potatoes, peeled and cut into quarters

Kernels cut from 2 fresh corn cobs (see page 88)

1 small, sturdy Scotch bonnet

3 sprigs of thyme

Sea salt

Handful of chopped coriander, to garnish

Continuing our journey around the world, let's visit Jamaica and the Rastafarian community, where 'ital' means 'vital'. Many words start with 'i' in the rastafarian dialect, to signify the unity of 'I' or 'eye' with God and nature. Rastas are mostly vegan; they try to live and eat naturally, with no processed food, sometimes no salt, using only clay or wood vessels. I made this stew for the funeral of my neighbours' father who was a Rastafarian. Authentic Caribbean funerals have nine nights of mourning, a tradition that started in Africa. On the ninth night, food and over-proofed rum are provided, and towards midnight, the spirit of the deceased is 'seen'. Family and friends sing, sending the spirit on its way.

You'll need some great Caribbean ingredients here. Yam has many varieties, some of which are nicer than others (I'm not keen on the slimier ones). For some reason Americans refer to sweet potatoes as yams. Cookbook writer Catherine Phipps, who spent a few months in the Caribbean, says the only way to buy a genuine Scotch bonnet is to smell it. She digs her thumbnail in to get at the flesh (hoping the shopkeeper won't notice!) and if it smells floral, it's genuine. Most of the time in the UK, Scotch bonnets are actually habaneros. Christophenes are also known as cho-cho or chayote. I've seen all these ingredients in big supermarkets and ethnic shops.

I hope you all 'overstand' this recipe, as Rastas would say! ('Understand' is considered rather negative.) The Ginger Cristophenes and Trinidadian Green Seasoning are both over the page, and brilliant dishes in themselves.

Heat the coconut oil in a large, heavy-bottomed saucepan, add the spring onions and garlic and fry until soft, then add the pimento berries, carrots and plantain. Stir, then add the black-eyed beans. Continue to cook over a low heat for 10 minutes, then add the coconut milk and vegetable stock, followed by the callaloo, yams or eddoes, sweet potatoes, sweetcorn and thyme.

Add salt to taste and cook over a low heat for about 30–40 minutes or until the potatoes and yams are soft enough to pierce with a fork. 15 minutes before the end of cooking, add the whole Scotch bonnet. Check the seasoning before serving, garnished with coriander. Accompany with Ginger Cristophenes and Trinidadian Green Seasoning (see page 146).

Ginger Christophenes

Serves 4

2 christophenes, thinly
sliced

2–3 tbsp coconut oil

5cm piece of ginger,
peeled and julienned

2 garlic cloves, very
finely chopped

1 sprig of thyme

3–5 spring onions,
chopped into 5cm
lengths

1 not-too-ripe pear,
cored and thinly
sliced (optional)

Sea salt

Christophenes, cho-chos or chayotes look a bit
like pears and have a subtle flavour, between a
melon and a cucumber, with a crisp texture. You'll
find them in ethnic shops and they are one of the
more popular Caribbean vegetables, but they are
also used in Asian and Mexican cooking.

Par-boil the christophene slices for
5 minutes in boiling, salted water, then
drain. Heat the coconut oil in a heavy-
bottomed frying pan and fry the christophene
slices with the ginger, garlic and thyme.
Add the spring onions with the pear, if
using, and season with salt.

Trinidadian Green Seasoning

3 whole garlic bulbs, roasted
(see page 141)

Bunch of thyme, leaves only

Bunch of coriander, leaves only

Handful of basil, leaves only

Bunch of chives

3 sprigs of oregano, leaves only

1 celery stick, roughly chopped

Handful of parsley, leaves only

2 green chillies, deseeded if you
don't want too much heat

5 spring onions, roughly chopped

1 green pepper, deseeded

Bunch of chadon beni, leaves only
(optional)

Juice of 1 lemon

1½ tbsp sea salt, or to taste

This green seasoning became a
favourite condiment of mine over
the course of writing this book; it
is equally good on toast, or with
chips. Chadon beni can be bought in
Chinese shops as 'sawtooth' or 'long
coriander', and it has a very strong
fresh coriander flavour.

Put all the ingredients into a
food processor and pulverise to
a paste.

Courgette Flowers with Mint & Apple Salad

Serves 4

For the apple salad:

3 tbsp cider vinegar

½ tsp brown sugar

1 tsp sea salt

2 crisp apples, cored and thinly sliced

For the flowers:

150g Smoky Chipotle Cashew Cheese (see page 33) or 8 tbsp vegan melty cheese

Handful of mint leaves, finely chopped, plus extra leaves to garnish

8 courgette flowers

Vegetable oil, for deep-frying

Maple syrup, for drizzling

For the batter:

200ml cold sparkling water

200g tempura flour OR 160g plain flour sifted with 40g cornflour

1 tsp sea salt

Edible flowers are a somewhat neglected part of the plant-based diet. With this recipe, you literally can't go wrong. People will be so impressed.

Prepare the apple salad by mixing the vinegar, sugar and salt together in a bowl. Then toss in the apple slices and chill in the fridge for an hour.

Mix the cheese and the mint together, then carefully unfurl the flowers (check for insects) and stuff a walnut-sized ball of stuffing inside each flower. Reshape the flowers to enclose the stuffing securely.

To make the batter, add the sparkling water to the flour and salt. Do not over-stir. Lumps are fine; they add interest.

Pour enough oil into a deep frying pan to deep-fry the courgette flowers. This is best done in a proper deep-fat fryer, or in a saucepan with tongs and kitchen paper to drain them on. Courgette flowers are expensive and delicate, so you don't want them to move about too much. They must be in oil just deep enough to cover them. Heat the oil to 180°C. Dip the courgette flowers into the thick batter, then carefully add to the hot oil and deep-fry until pale golden.

Remove to a plate and drizzle some maple syrup on top. Serve with a small portion of the apple salad and some mint leaves.

Watermelon Stir-Fry with Rice

Serves 4

3 tbsp sesame oil

3 garlic cloves, very finely chopped

2.5cm piece of ginger, peeled and cut into fine strips

1 red onion, halved and sliced

2 tsp soy sauce

2 tbsp hoisin sauce

1 tsp sea salt

½ tsp freshly ground black pepper

100g mangetout

100g baby corn

400g watermelon, skin and rind removed (see note below), cut into 1cm-thick wedges

1 tbsp sweet chilli sauce

Coriander leaves, to garnish

Rice, to serve

Note:
Do not discard the rind of the watermelon — the white part between the red and the green skin — as it can be used to make pickles, southern Dolly-Parton style (see page 24). Or you could toss the rind in, separately, at the beginning; it is a little like cooked marrow.

Despite exhortations from the great and the good to be a 'locavore', sourcing fruit and veg locally, I must admit to a recent obsession with the tropics. Take watermelons, for instance. They're almost camp as a fruit, the outsize prehistoric green bowling ball with its juicy pink interior studded with black seeds. No artist can resist painting them. But they are a pain in the bicep to shop for... you need serious muscles to carry them, or have them delivered.

This is an unusual use of watermelon, but I do like the contrast of sweet, crisp red flesh with savoury Chinese flavours. Other uses for any leftover watermelon flesh include freezing and blitzing it to make watermelon cocktails.

Heat the sesame oil in a wok or a heavy-bottomed saucepan and throw in the garlic, ginger and onion. Fry for 5 minutes or so, then add the soy sauce, hoisin sauce, salt, pepper, mangetout, baby corn, watermelon and sweet chilli sauce. Fry over a high heat, moving the ingredients around rapidly but carefully with a wooden spoon.

Garnish with coriander leaves and serve with rice.

Cornbread & Gravy with Portobello Steaks

Serves 4

For the cornbread:

175ml unsweetened soya milk

2 tbsp cider vinegar

1 tsp egg replacer

1 tbsp water

175g cornmeal (NOT cornflour) or polenta

100g plain flour

50g brown sugar

1 tsp bicarbonate of soda

1 tsp sea salt

45ml vegetable oil, plus extra for oiling

Kernels cut from 2 fresh corn cobs (optional) (see page 88)

For the mushrooms:

2 tbsp vegan margarine

2 garlic cloves, very finely chopped

Handful of flat-leaf parsley, finely chopped

Pinch of sea salt

4 large portobello mushrooms

Freshly ground black pepper

For the gravy:

20g dried mushrooms

1 tbsp vegetable stock powder

35ml olive oil

2 shallots, finely chopped

2 garlic cloves, very finely chopped

100g fresh mushrooms, thinly sliced

2 tbsp dark soy sauce (or Braggs Liquid Aminos or Maggi Liquid Seasoning)

125ml glass of vegan red wine

3 tbsp plain flour

Freshly ground black pepper

I love cornbread. In this one I've added fresh corn for extra texture. Serve with gravy and grilled portobello mushrooms.

Preheat the oven to 200°C/gas mark 6.

Create the buttermilk equivalent by combining the soya milk and cider vinegar and letting sit for 10 minutes.

Combine the egg replacer with the water, then mix all the cornbread ingredients together. It will be quite liquid. For chunkier cornbread, include the sweetcorn kernels. Tip the mixture into an oiled ovenproof cast-iron skillet and bake in the oven for 30—40 minutes until golden and a skewer inserted into the middle comes out clean.

For the mushrooms, mix together the vegan margarine, garlic, parsley, salt and plenty of pepper, and cover the brown gills of each mushroom with it.

For the gravy, put the dried mushrooms and stock powder in a ½-litre heatproof jug and fill with boiling water. Set aside to soak for 30 minutes.

Heat the oil in a medium saucepan over a medium-high heat, add the shallots and cook until softened, then add the garlic and the fresh mushrooms. Add the soy sauce and red wine and cook until hot but not boiling, then stir in the flour very rapidly. Add the dried mushrooms and most of the soaking stock, and season with black pepper. Keep the gravy on a low simmer, adding more soaking stock if it gets too thick. (This gravy is great on virtually anything, including mashed potatoes.)

Preheat the grill to hot and grill the portobello mushrooms until they are hot all the way through and the garlic mixture is bubbling. Serve with hunks of cornbread and the gravy.

Jamaican Rice & Peas with Fresh Coconut

Serves 6

200g dried black-eyed, pinto or black turtle beans

½ onion, peeled

2 garlic cloves, peeled — 1 whole and 1 sliced

4–6 pimento (allspice) berries

2 spring onions, finely sliced

½ red pepper, deseeded and sliced

50–75g creamed coconut

2–3 fresh sprigs of or 1 tbsp dried thyme

1 tbsp soy sauce

1 Scotch bonnet chilli

½ fresh coconut, peeled and sliced (see page 18)

2 small slices of fresh ginger

500g basmati rice

1 tbsp coconut oil

Sea salt and freshly ground black pepper

My neighbour Karen, also a single mum, who comes from a Jamaican background, has started a sideline in selling proper Jamaican food to other mums outside the school gate. She's named herself Msricenpeas. Parents are flocking to buy tubs of her rice and peas, callaloo and jerk chicken. I can't blame them — it's delicious, healthy and, whilst seemingly simple, it's time-consuming to make properly.

Rice and peas is the mainstay food of Jamaican cuisine. 'Peas' are beans, and the further south, the darker the legume. Caribbean islands near to the Southern States of America will often use the black-eyed pea as I have. Jamaicans use the pinto bean. Islands closer to South America will use the small black turtle bean. The smaller the pea, the sweeter it is.

Karen kindly gave me her recipe. A couple of pointers: it surprised me that she soaked the peas with garlic and onion 'to soften them'. Softening those peas is important. And I had some fresh coconut, so I cooked my peas with a few large slices. It lent a rich depth to the flavour.

Soak the beans in filtered or cooled boiled water from the kettle, overnight if possible, adding the onion and whole garlic clove halfway through (yes, I have woken up in the night to put onion and garlic in my beans). Drain, discard the onion and garlic and tip the beans into a heavy pot or casserole.

Add the pimento berries and sliced garlic and cover everything with boiling water. Simmer over a low heat for 45 minutes, then add the spring onions and red pepper and simmer until the beans are cooked. Don't let them get too soft; they should smell sweet and creamy.

Pour just enough hot water over the creamed coconut to dissolve, then add to the beans. You can add more or less if you prefer; I find too much coconut cream makes the rice greasy. Add the thyme, soy sauce, whole Scotch bonnet, fresh coconut and ginger and simmer, covered, for 15 minutes. Then fish out and discard the whole Scotch bonnet. Wash the rice and, once it is free of starch, add it to the beans and stir with a fork. Add about 1 litre water and the coconut oil. Add salt and pepper to taste and cook, covered, over a low heat (or in the oven at 160°C/gas mark 2½) until the rice is soft and fluffy, checking on the water levels but without stirring. Enjoy!

Wild Mushroom Forest Pie

Serves 6—8

For the pastry:

500g plain flour

1 tsp sea salt

150ml olive oil,
   semi-frozen
   (see recipe
   introduction)

60—80ml iced water

1 tbsp cider
   vinegar

**For the mushroom
   filling:**

40ml olive oil

3 shallots, very
   finely chopped

2 garlic cloves,
   very finely chopped

750g wild mushrooms

100ml soya cream

200ml vermouth or
   vegan white wine

A dozen stemmed
   mushrooms for
   decoration,
   e.g. enoki

Vegan margarine,
   melted, for
   brushing

Unsweetened almond
   or soya milk,
   to glaze

Sea salt and
   freshly ground
   black pepper

In the States, Isa Chandra Moskowitz and Terry Hope Romero are THE vegan cookbook authors. They've known each other for 20 years, meeting on the New York punk scene. I asked Terry if I could nick her recipe for vegan pie crust. It's really quite ingenious. Rather than using butter or shortening, use partially frozen olive oil. Just freeze in a plastic container for a couple of hours before using it.

To make the pastry, sift the flour and salt into a large bowl. Working quickly so that it stays cold, add the olive oil by the tablespoonful, cutting it into the flour with your fingers or a pastry cutter, until the mixture appears pebbly. Mix 60ml iced water with the vinegar and drizzle 2 tbsp into the flour. Stir into the dough, adding more liquid 1 tbsp at a time until it holds together to form a soft ball; you may not need all of the iced water. Take care not to over-work the dough. (You can make the pastry in a food processor if you prefer.)

Divide the dough in half and roll into balls, then press each into a flat disc. Wrap each in clingfilm and leave to rest in the fridge for 30 minutes.

Heat the olive oil for the filling in a frying pan over a medium heat, add the shallots and garlic and sweat for 20 minutes, or until soft. Add the mushrooms, soya cream and vermouth or wine and cook until thick. Season and set aside to cool. Meanwhile, preheat the oven to 200°C/gas mark 6.

Roll out both discs of pastry to the thickness of a pound coin, to fit the bottom and top of your pie dish (approximately 20cm x 20cm). Fit the bottom crust into the pie dish, add the cooled filling and gently press down to get everything in. Cover with the top crust, pinch the edges together to seal, trim any excess dough and crimp the edges with the tines of a fork. Make 5 slits in the top of the pie and poke the mushroom stems into them (the holes also help steam escape). Brush the top of the mushrooms with a little vegan margarine and brush the pie with the milk.

Cover the pie with foil and bake for 20 minutes. Reduce the oven temperature to 180°C/gas mark 4 and bake for 30 more minutes or until the filling bubbles up through the edges, removing the foil for the last 15 minutes so that the top will go golden.

Nut Roast

This dish has such
a bad reputation I
almost feared to
tackle it. It sums
up every cliché
about vegetarian or
vegan food: brown,
wholesome, heavy.
But you'll find that
despite its worthy
appearance, this
recipe has a stalwart
fan club, even
amongst meat eaters.
Sandwiched inside the
basic nut roast in my
recipe, there are two
alternative fillings:
one with traditional
Christmassy vegetables
and another with a
spicier Malaysian feel
if you want something
a little different.

For the filling (2 alternatives):

Filling One (traditional Christmas dinner):

200g parsnips, peeled and halved lengthways

200g Jerusalem artichokes, peeled and halved

100ml olive oil

Several sprigs of rosemary

1 tbsp ground cumin

2 tbsp sea salt

▼▾■■▾■◆▾◗■◆■◆◆■■◆◗■■■■■■■■■■■▾■◗▾◆■◆▾■■■■◗◗◆

Preheat the oven to 200°C/gas mark 6.

Put the parsnips and artichokes into a baking
tray and pour the olive oil over them, tossing
them with your hands so that they are well
covered. Snip some rosemary leaves over and
sprinkle the over the cumin, then the sea salt.
Roast in the oven for 35 minutes until golden.

Filling Two:

2 red peppers, deseeded and cut into
    thin strips

6 tomatoes, diced

75ml olive oil

1 dried red chilli

½ fresh coconut, peeled and ground in a food
    processor or finely chopped (see page 18)

Sea salt

▼▾■■◆■◆■■◗▾◗■◆▾◗■◗■◆◆◗■■■■■■■■■◗■◗◆▾■◆◆▾◆■◆■◗■■◗

Fry the peppers and tomatoes together in the
oil until the peppers are soft. Crumble over
the dried chilli, taking care not to add the
seeds if you don't want it too hot. Add the
finely chopped coconut, and salt to taste, and
fry for a few minutes.

For the nut roast:

50ml olive oil, for frying and oiling

4 shallots or 2 onions, diced

Cloves of 1 whole garlic bulb, very finely chopped

400g cashew nuts or 200g cashews and 200g macadamia nuts

300g sourdough breadcrumbs (for a gluten-free version, use brown rice)

200ml vegetable stock

Juice of ½ lemon

50g almonds or pecan nuts

Sea salt and freshly ground black pepper

Fresh herbs, to garnish

Heat some olive oil in a frying pan over a medium heat and add the shallots or onions with the garlic. Soften until translucent and sweet.

Preheat the oven to 200°C/gas mark 6.

Grind the nuts in a blender, food processor or by hand, leaving some whole to add interest to the texture, if you like. Mix together the ground nuts, breadcrumbs, fried shallot or onion and garlic mixture, the vegetable stock, lemon juice and salt and pepper to taste.

Oil a 1kg loaf tin and line with baking parchment. Neatly place the almonds or pecan nuts all over the bottom — when the nut roast is turned out, they will be the decoration on top. Put half the nut roast mixture into the tin. Top with one of the filling options. If using the parsnips and artichokes, then lay the parsnips lengthways along the loaf tin, dotted with the artichokes. If using the pepper, tomato and coconut filling, just spread it on top.

Add the rest of the nut roast mixture to the top, cover with foil and bake for 30 minutes. Remove the foil and bake for another 10 minutes until the top is dark golden. Leave to cool in the tin for 30 minutes.

Turn the loaf out onto a decorative plate. Garnish with fresh herbs and serve by the slice.

Spectacular Russian Stuffed Cabbage Rose

Serves 4

A recipe adapted from *A Taste of Russia* (by Darra Goldstein): whole stuffed baked cabbage. As the original was with meat, I made up my own. It looks terribly pretty unfurled as you stuff the filling inside each leaf. And later, once cooked, it resembles a Christmas pudding, so it makes a festive vegan centrepiece. You can also do this with mini cabbages, one per person, in which case adjust the recipe accordingly.

1 Savoy cabbage

200g red quinoa

50ml olive oil, plus extra for brushing and oiling

2 white onions, finely diced

100g wild or brown mushrooms, chopped

1 tsp ground cumin

100g dill, plus extra to garnish

300g frozen cranberries, plus extra to garnish

3 tbsp sugar

300ml soya cream

Sea salt and freshly ground black pepper

Boil or steam the cabbage by plunging it whole into boiling, salted water in a large saucepan. Cook for around 15 minutes or until still firm but tender. Remove from the pan and leave to cool.

Preheat the oven to 180°C/gas mark 4.

Rinse the quinoa in a sieve until the water runs clear. Use double the volume of water to quinoa — in this case 400ml water — and put both in a medium saucepan with 1 tsp salt. Bring to the boil, then cook for about 20 minutes. Leave to stand for 5 minutes off the heat and with the lid on. Then uncover and fluff it up with a fork.

Heat the olive oil in a pan, add the onions and cook until softened, then add the mushrooms, cumin, dill and salt and pepper to taste. Add a third of the cranberries and 1 tbsp of the sugar and cook until they break down. Mix the drained quinoa with the cranberry mixture. Take your cooled cabbage and carefully open out the leaves (it looks like a flower when you serve it).

Brush all the leaves with olive oil seasoned with salt and pepper. Using a dessertspoon, pack a spoonful of mixture into the base of each leaf. When finished, pull all the leaves up and close the cabbage. Tie to secure with kitchen string and place on an oiled baking tray. Brush the top of the cabbage with oil and bake for 30 minutes, then remove from the oven and cover the cabbage with the soya cream. Return it to the oven and bake for another 10–15 minutes.

Meanwhile, put the rest of the cranberries and sugar in a saucepan over a medium-high heat. Cook until the sugar has dissolved and the berries start to go mushy.

Place the baked cabbage whole on a serving plate and snip off the string. Garnish with extra cranberries and some dill. It can then be sliced like a cake.

Roast Parsnips & Jerusalem Artichokes

Serves 4–6

Sugar-sweet roast veg with added cumin to combat flatulence, which might help with the 'fartichokes'. I can't guarantee it, though.

1.5kg parsnips, peeled and trimmed

1kg Jerusalem artichokes, peeled

75ml olive oil

1 tbsp sea salt

1 tsp cumin seeds

Freshly ground black pepper

Preheat the oven to 190°C/gas mark 5. Place the parsnips and artichokes in a roasting tin and toss them in the olive oil and salt. Bake for 45 minutes or until golden. Add the cumin and some black pepper.

Aubergine Baked with Miso Glaze

Serves 4

Serve this simple main or side from Japan, known as *nasu dengaku*, with sushi rice or noodles, the green bean dish (see page 121) and some pickles. Miso is a very healthy fermented foodstuff; some even claim that it combats radiation sickness.

2 tbsp mirin

2 tbsp sake or rice wine

4 tbsp white miso

2 tbsp brown sugar

2 large, shiny, firm aubergines

4 tsp sesame oil

For the garnish:

Toasted sesame seeds

Spring onions, green part only, cut into 4cm lengths

Preheat the oven to 190°C/gas mark 5.

Place the mirin and sake or rice wine in a small saucepan and bring to a simmer over a medium heat. Simmer for about 2 minutes, then add the miso and stir until smooth. Stir in the sugar and reduce the heat to very low.

Cut the aubergines in half lengthways. Score the flesh side of each aubergine half with a crisscross diamond pattern and brush with the sesame oil. Place, cut side down, on a baking tray and bake in the oven for 10 minutes.

Heat the grill to very hot. Turn the aubergines over and place under the hot grill for about 5 minutes. You want them just light brown, soft inside and slightly crispy on top.

Spoon the miso sauce onto the cut sides and put them back under the grill for another minute until the sauce bubbles. Sprinkle with toasted sesame seeds and spring onions and serve.

Roast Potatoes in Coconut Oil

Serves 4

Coconut oil has a high smoking point, which means that you get crispy fluffy roast potatoes every time. There is a rule about roast potatoes — people will always want more and there are never enough. So do more than you think is necessary. And don't hold back on the fat and salt.

▼▪▪▪▪▪▪▪▪◀▪▪▪▪▪▌▪▪▪▪▪▪▪▪▪

2kg floury potatoes, peeled and cut into quarters or similar sizes

3 tbsp coconut oil

50ml olive oil

Sea salt

Preheat the oven to 200°C/gas mark 6. Par-boil the potatoes for 10 minutes in a large saucepan of boiling, salted water. Drain and tip into a roasting tin, shaking the potatoes to 'chuff' them.

Add the coconut oil, olive oil and salt to taste. Turn to coat the potatoes, then bake for 45 minutes or until golden and crispy, giving the tin a shake halfway through the cooking time.

Variations:

Originally, potatoes were from the New World, specifically the Peruvian Andes. So I've come up with some interesting flavour combinations (which can be applied to most roast vegetables) to liven up the Sunday roast or Christmas dinner.

Tropical: Roast slices of blood orange with the potatoes. Add fresh coconut, cut into 5mm strips, just before the end as it cooks more quickly. Garnish with coriander pesto or dried chilli flakes.

Italian: My Italian great-grandmother Nanny Savino taught this recipe to my very British mother. Pour a tin of tomatoes onto the potatoes and mix it in. Add a few cloves of garlic and crumble some oregano onto it.

Middle Eastern: Add garlic, sumac, harissa, cumin and coriander seeds to the potatoes.

Saffron: Add a large pinch of saffron strands to the par-boiling water.

Wilted Day Lilies with Mustard Greens

Serves 4

2–3 tbsp olive oil

1kg mustard greens
  or other dark
  greens, washed,
  stems cut out if
  they are thick

2 garlic cloves,
  very finely chopped

1 red chilli,
  deseeded and finely
  sliced

8–10 day lilies,
  stamens removed

Sea salt

Steamed rice or
  boiled tapioca,
  to serve

Day lilies are incredibly sweet, like honey.
Pick unsprayed ones once they have opened for
those brief few hours. Remove the stamens and
make sure there are no insects.

Heat the oil in a large frying pan over a
medium-high heat. Add the mustard or other
greens, garlic and chilli, with sea salt
to taste. After 5 or so minutes when the
greens are wilted, add the day lilies on
top and let them wilt also.

Serve the lilies hot with steamed rice or
boiled tapioca.

Artichoke, Potato, Spinach & Tofu B'stilla with Poppy Seeds & Rose Petals

Serves 6–8

One of the most stunning meals I've ever had was at a Moroccan restaurant in LA. We were served vast platters with pyramids of couscous and a b'stilla, an exotic filled pastry pie. Try this easy vegan b'stilla, an explosion of sweet and savoury.

2 large potatoes, peeled

Olive oil, for frying, oiling and brushing

1 onion, sliced

2 garlic cloves, sliced

1 cinnamon stick

500g fresh spinach

400g firm tofu, drained and cut into 2.5cm squares

400g tin of artichoke hearts, drained and halved

50g flaked almonds

30g green sultanas (available from Indian shops)

1 tbsp sugar

20g pine nuts

1 tbsp ras el hanout spice mix

1 tsp harissa

1–2 preserved lemons, cut into small pieces

Handful of black olives, stoned

4 large sheets of filo pastry

Poppy seeds, for sprinkling

Icing sugar, for dusting

Sea salt

Rose petals, to garnish

Boil the potatoes in a medium saucepan, with 1 tsp salt in the water, for 15–20 minutes until just tender. Drain and cut into 2.5cm chunks.

Heat some olive oil in a large saucepan over a medium heat, add the onion and cook until soft. Add the garlic, cinnamon stick, potatoes, 1 tbsp sea salt and the spinach. Let the spinach cook down, then add the tofu. Add the artichoke hearts, almonds, sultanas, sugar, pine nuts, ras el hanout and harissa. Finally, add the preserved lemons and olives. Remove the pan from the heat and let it cool.

Preheat the oven to 200°C/gas mark 6. To make the b'stilla, remove the base from a deep, 18cm springform cake tin (you need just the sides/ring as a support) and place on an oiled baking tray. Working with one piece of filo at a time and keeping the rest covered with a damp tea towel, to prevent them from drying out, brush the sheet with olive oil and place it in the centre of the tin, draping it over the sides. Then brush a second piece of filo and lay it on top, at an angle to the first. Do this with all 4 sheets until the base and tin sides are completely covered with the pastry, with the excess overhanging the sides.

Put the cooled filling mixture in the middle and fold over the overhanging filo to cover the top. Brush the top with olive oil and sprinkle with poppy seeds. Cover with foil and put the baking tray, with the tin sides/ring, into the oven. Bake for 30 minutes, removing the foil after 25 minutes to let the top get crispy.

Remove from the oven, remove the springform sides/ring and transfer the b'stilla to a serving plate, using a spatula. Dust the top with icing sugar and sprinkle with rose petals and some more black poppy seeds.

Dessert

In some ways, dessert,
so often about dairy and
eggs, is the hardest course
for the plant-based diet.
But amazing puddings can
be achieved using vegan-
friendly ingredients.

Black & Green Cheesecake
with Bengali Lime & Avocado

Serves 6—8

Oil spray, for greasing

For the crust:

150g Oreo cookies, finely
    ground

3 tbsp coconut milk

For the filling:

150g cashew nuts, soaked
    in water for 2—4 hours,
    then drained

2 small avocados, peeled
    and stoned

½ tsp sea salt

1 tsp vanilla paste or
    1 vanilla pod, split
    lengthways

100ml agave nectar

Juice of 2 lemons

100ml coconut oil

Juice of 5 limes, plus the
    pared zest of 1 for the
    top (optional)

Slices of kiwi fruit,
    for the top (optional)

Key limes or Mexican limes used in Key
lime pie are very different from the usual
'Persian' limes that we know in our shops.
Key limes are smaller, more acidic and the
flesh is yellow. Once dried into black lime,
they are a useful ingredient in Middle
Eastern cookery. The strange thing about
both Key limes and Persian limes is that
they are ripe when yellow, not green.

As it's hard to get hold of Key limes in
this country, I use normal limes. But if
you can get hold of Bengali limes (I buy
them at Asian supermarkets, especially in
Whitechapel), then do. They are perfumed,
floral and exotic.

Preheat the oven to 180°C/gas mark 4
and lightly spray an 18cm loose-
bottomed cake tin with oil spray.

In a mixing bowl, combine the ground
Oreos and coconut milk. Press the
mixture into the bottom of the cake
tin. Chill in the fridge for about
30 minutes.

Put all the ingredients except the lime
zest and kiwi fruit into a powerful
blender. Process until smooth. Then
take the cheesecake base from the
fridge and ladle in the green filling.

Decorate with curls of pared lime
zest, or with overlapping layers of
kiwi fruit slices, or both. Chill in
the fridge for 2 hours before serving.

Chocolate, Orange, Chestnut & Tofu Mousse with Coconut Yoghurt & Marinated Blood Oranges

Serves 4

1 blood orange

30ml Cointreau

150g vegan orange dark or dark chocolate, broken into pieces

300g very soft silken tofu, at room temperature

250g tin of sweetened crème de marrons (chestnut purée)

Glug of Cointreau or Triple Sec liqueur (optional)

Plain coconut milk yoghurt (e.g. CoYo), to serve

This is just as rich and velvety as a dairy chocolate mousse and frankly easier to make. If you don't have blood oranges, use normal ones.

Pare a couple of strips of zest off the orange and set aside for later. Then completely peel the orange and cut a small slice from the bottom and top of the orange so that it sits on a board. Using a sharp, flexible knife, carefully remove the white pith, cutting from top to bottom around the orange and trying to retain the shape of the orange. Turn the orange on its side and cut into thin rounds. Put into a bowl, add the Cointreau and leave for a few hours.

Melt the chocolate in the microwave on full power in 30-second bursts. Do not do it for longer bursts or it will ruin (or 'seize') the chocolate. Good chocolate is expensive.

Put the melted chocolate in a powerful blender with the tofu and crème de marrons and blend until smooth. Add a shot of Cointreau or Triple Sec if you wish.

Divide the mousse between 4 serving glasses or ramekins and refrigerate for 2 hours. Decorate the top with a slice or two of the marinated blood orange, the pared zest and some coconut milk yoghurt.

Rhubarb Crumble with Custard

Serves 6–8

1kg rhubarb, cut into
    5cm lengths

100g caster sugar

1 tsp ground ginger

½ tsp ground cinnamon

½ tsp ground nutmeg

For the crumble:

100g rolled oats

100g plain flour

100g brown sugar

1 tsp ground cinnamon

½ tsp sea salt

50g coconut oil

The perfect winter pudding, a British classic.

Preheat the oven to 180°C/gas mark 4 and oil an ovenproof dish about 24cm x 17cm.

Mix together the rhubarb, caster sugar, ginger, cinnamon and nutmeg and tip into the prepared dish. Cover with foil and bake for 15 minutes. Remove from the oven and set aside.

In a bowl, combine the oats, flour, brown sugar, cinnamon and salt. Then, with cool hands, rub the coconut oil into this mixture until it resembles breadcrumbs.

Remove the foil from the rhubarb dish and sprinkle the crumble over the rhubarb. Bake for 30–40 minutes or until golden. Serve hot with the custard below.

Custard

Serves 6–8

2 tbsp potato starch

2 tbsp cornflour

800ml rice or nut milk

100g sugar

2 vanilla pods, split
    lengthways and seeds
    scraped out, or
    2 tsp vanilla paste

This works and tastes pretty good. It does also work with soya milk, but I prefer the flavour of rice or nut milk.

Put the potato starch and cornflour into a saucepan and add a little of the milk, stirring to make a paste.

Warm the remaining milk in a heavy-bottomed saucepan over a low heat, whisking in the sugar and vanilla until the sugar has dissolved. Stir with a wooden spoon for at least 5 minutes or until the custard becomes slightly transparent. It's important to cook out the starchy flavour of the flour.

Once you can run your finger down the wooden spoon and you can see the wood, take the custard off the heat and serve.

Roast Peaches with Lavender & Coconut Salted Caramel

Serves 4–6

6 ripe peaches, halved and stoned

Lavender sugar, for sprinkling

Lavender flowers, to decorate (optional)

For the coconut salted caramel:

400ml tin of coconut milk

50g brown sugar

Pinch of good-quality sea salt, such as fleur de sel or Maldon

Choose ripe, in-season peaches for this.

To make the coconut salted caramel, heat the coconut milk and sugar in a wide-bottomed saucepan over a very low heat for an hour or so until it caramelises and thickens. Stir occasionally. Then transfer to a jug, adding a little sea salt. Meanwhile, preheat the oven to 180°C/gas mark 4.

Place the peach halves cut side up in a roasting tin and sprinkle with lavender sugar. Roast for 30 minutes.

Scoop a couple of tablespoons of the salted caramel into each bowl, then top with 2–3 roasted peach halves. Garnish with a few fresh lavender flowers, if you like.

Chia Seed, Rose & Raspberry Falooda

Serves 4

4 tbsp chia seeds

400ml sweetened almond or
rice milk, chilled

4 tbsp caster or coconut
sugar

8 scoops of vegan vanilla
ice cream

400g raspberries

4 tsp rosewater

Mint leaves, to garnish

This is an Indian 'sundae' traditionally made with basil seeds, which expand and have a soft gelatinous texture with a nutty centre. A falooda can alternatively be made with vermicelli, which is something most Westerners are not too keen on — it's like rice pudding, but with pasta. So I've eliminated the vermicelli. Chia seeds are a healthy update, for chia lowers cholesterol and adds fibre to the diet.

Soak the chia seeds in the milk and sugar for at least 15 minutes.

Divide the mixture between 4 tall glasses, then add a scoop of ice cream, a few raspberries, 1 tsp rosewater, another scoop of ice cream and more raspberries. Finally, top with a few mint leaves.

Vegan Brownies with Cinnamon or Kahlúa Cream

Serves 10

2 tbsp ground flaxseed
(golden linseed)

150g plain flour

60g cocoa powder

300g caster sugar

100g cinnamon sugar

½ tsp baking powder

1 tsp good-quality sea
salt, ideally fleur de
sel (this gives it a
lovely flavour)

120ml water

100ml sweetened almond
or hazelnut milk

280ml rapeseed or
groundnut oil, plus
extra for oiling
(optional)

1 tbsp vanilla extract or
1 Mexican vanilla pod,
ground

1 tbsp chipotle paste

1 tsp smoked paprika

100g vegan orange dark
chocolate, chopped
(Plamil does a nice
one)

170g pecan nuts

To serve:

Soya cream

Sprinkling of ground
cinnamon or Kahlúa

These are fudgy, light and moreish. Even
non-brownie lovers love them. I got the
basic recipe from Ms. Cupcake, the Brixton-
based vegan bakery, but I've gone further by
Mexicanising them and making them richer.

Preheat the oven to 180°C/gas mark 4.
Oil a baking tin, 33cm x 23cm, or line
with baking parchment.

In a cup, whisk the flaxseed with 2 tbsp
lukewarm water and leave to soak. In a
large bowl or stand mixer, combine the
flour, cocoa, caster sugar, cinnamon
sugar, baking powder and salt. Then
add the water, nut milk, oil, vanilla,
chipotle paste, smoked paprika, orange
chocolate, the flaxseed mixture and half
the pecans.

Mix well, then pour into the prepared
tin. Arrange the remaining pecans on
top of the brownie mixture and bake in
the oven for 20 minutes. The brownie
may not look cooked when it comes out,
but it sets as it cools. You want a
soft gooey inside. Leave in the tin
to cool, then cut into sections.
Serve with soya cream sprinkled with
cinnamon or streaked through with a
swig of Kahlúa.

No one will know they are vegan. Shh!

Passionfruit & Rosewater Pavlova!

Serves 4–6

For the meringue:

100g egg replacer

250ml water

125g icing sugar

1 tbsp rosewater

For the topping:

500ml passionfruit juice

200g caster sugar

4 ripe passionfruit
(they should be wrinkly)

2 quantities Coconut
Whipped Cream (see page
30) or Soyatoo Soy Whip,
whipped

I was amazed how well egg replacers work
to create something that I thought was
intrinsically about egg whites. Try it.

Preheat the oven to 110°C/gas mark ¼.
Whisk the egg replacer with the water
in a stand mixer at top speed, or in
a bowl using an electric whisk, for
at least 5 minutes until soft peaks
form. Then slowly add the icing sugar,
whisking it in for another 5 minutes or
until glossy. Stir in the rosewater.

Line a baking sheet with a silicone
baking mat or baking parchment. Pipe
or scoop the meringue mixture onto the
baking sheet and create a slight dip
in the middle. Bake for 2 hours.

Let it cool on the baking sheet, then
carefully remove the baking mat or
baking parchment and transfer the
meringue to a platter.

Put the passionfruit juice in a medium
saucepan and reduce to a syrup over a
medium-high heat. Let it cool. Then
cut open the passionfruit and scoop the
pulp out into the syrup.

Assemble the pavlova by scooping a
billowing layer of Coconut Whipped
Cream or whipped Soy Whip into the dip
in the middle of the meringue, then
pouring the syrup on top, letting it
drip over the sides.

Pâte de Fruits

Serves 4

This recipe lends itself to all kinds of flavours and alcohols. There are some unusual ingredients (pectin, glucose syrup and citric acid), but it's worth buying them for future use, as they don't cost much, don't go off and you can use them for many other recipes. Try flavours like passionfruit, quince, or as I've done here, blackcurrant. And try adding Champagne for a 'kir royale'-flavoured pâte de fruits.

12g yellow pectin (available online at www.souschef.co.uk or www.melburyandappleton. co.uk)

550g caster sugar

500g blackcurrant or other flavoured purée, such as passionfruit (buy it or make your own, see right)

70g glucose syrup

3g citric acid (available at Lakeland or in Asian food stores)

100g granulated sugar, for dusting

Equipment:

Digital thermometer

Plastic container, 10cm x 20cm, lined with enough clingfilm to hang over the sides

Mix the pectin and 50g of the caster sugar together in a small bowl or cup. Have this next to your hob.

Heat the purée in a medium, heavy-bottomed saucepan to medium-hot, then whisk in the pectin and sugar mixture. Bring to the boil, then tip in the remaining 500g caster sugar and the glucose syrup. Measuring on a thermometer, bring the mixture to 107°C and continue to boil at that temperature for a few minutes until it appears to be thicker than jam.

Take off the heat and add the citric acid, then pour into the plastic container to set. Chill in the fridge for 1 hour or until set, then unmould and cut into diamonds or cubes.

Pour the granulated sugar into a shallow dish and turn the diamonds or cubes in it to coat liberally.

To make blackcurrant purée:

Blend 500g blackcurrants (frozen if not in season) with 100g caster sugar and 3 tbsp lemon juice. Then push through a sieve to remove all the seeds.
Put this in a medium, heavy-bottomed saucepan and warm until the sugar has dissolved and the fruit has thickened slightly. Remove from the heat, allow to cool and then set aside until ready to use. This will keep in the freezer for 3 months.

Blueberry Soup

Serves 4

500g fresh
  or frozen
  blueberries

350ml water

60–75g caster
  sugar,
  depending on
  how sweet you
  like it

Juice of ½ lemon

1 glass of vegan
  sweet white
  dessert wine
  or Madeira
  (optional)

2 tbsp cornflour

This is a dish I discovered on a trip to Sweden, although the hot fruit soup is also a thing in Eastern Europe. As well as the blueberries, blackberries, raspberries and strawberries, the Swedes can forage for cloudberries, bilberries, lingonberries and seabuckthorn berries. Berries are considered a superfood, full of antioxidants and vitamin C, plus anti-ageing properties. The Swedes, in the summer, serve refreshing and healthy fruit soups with bilberries or rose hips, but I love blueberries.

Slowly simmer the blueberries, water, sugar and lemon juice together. Once the blueberries have started to disintegrate, continue to simmer, adding the sweet wine if you wish. Then strain the soup, pushing it through a sieve with a wooden spoon.

Mix the cornflour to a paste with a few tablespoons of water. Add this to the warm, sieved blueberry soup. You could then put it through a blender to make it even smoother. Serve warm or cold.

Orange Flower Water, Cardamom & Coconut Rice Pudding

Serves 2–3

Coconut oil,
  for oiling

80g pudding rice

100g caster sugar

400ml tin of
  coconut milk

300ml water

2 tbsp orange
  flower water

5 green cardamom
  pods

A highly perfumed version of a classic pud.

Preheat the oven to 160°C/gas mark 2½.

Use a little coconut oil to lightly oil a shallow ovenproof dish, about 20cm x 20cm. Combine the rice, sugar and coconut milk in a large bowl. Add the water (you can put it in the tin of coconut milk, rinsing out the last bits of coconut).

Stir, then transfer to the prepared dish and add the orange flower water and cardamom pods. Bake for 1 hour 30 minutes, stirring 3 or 4 times during cooking, until the rice is tender.

Put the dish under a hot grill for 10 minutes to get a brown skin on top. Serve hot or cold.

Three Cherry Swiss Roll Trifle

Serves 4–6

For the Swiss roll:

260g self-raising flour

2 tsp baking powder

1 tsp sea salt

2 ripe bananas, peeled

Juice of 1 lemon

220g caster sugar, plus
2 tbsp for sprinkling

1 tsp vanilla paste

100ml olive oil

120ml water

For the filling:

200g vegan margarine

150g icing sugar

150g tinned or frozen
sour cherries, drained
and stoned

For the jelly:

400ml cherry juice

200g caster sugar

100g cherries, stoned

200ml sloe gin, Malibu or
cherry brandy

2 level tsp agar agar
powder

To assemble:

150g morello or black
cherries, pitted

250ml vegan whipped cream
(from a can is best)

50g fresh cherries, left
whole with stems

Icing sugar, for dusting

Yes, you can make vegan trifle. The jelly is set with agar agar, so do pay attention to how many grams of agar powder you put in, otherwise it sets as solid as a rock, which isn't what you want in a jelly. There is also a split between those who think the jelly should be on top and others who believe the jelly should be the bottom layer. One could write a PhD on this kind of thing.

Sour cherries aren't easy to get hold of, but you can buy them tinned, in a jar or frozen from Middle Eastern suppliers.

As you assemble, make sure the coils of Swiss roll can be seen through the sides of the glass bowl. This should be a billowing froufrou dessert in red and white.

You will need a Swiss roll tin, or a baking tray plus non-stick baking parchment.

Obviously the Swiss roll and the jelly can also be served as separate desserts.

Preheat the oven to 200°C/gas mark 6. Line a Swiss roll tin or baking tray with good-quality baking parchment.

Combine the flour, baking powder and salt in a bowl and set aside. Then in another bowl or in your stand mixer, beat together the bananas, lemon juice and sugar, then beat in the vanilla paste and olive oil. The mixture should be fluffy.

Gradually fold the flour mixture and the water into the creamed banana mixture, then pour into the lined tin and spread it flat with a palette knife. Bake in the oven for 10–12 minutes or until the top is springy to the touch.

Remove it from the oven and clear a space on your worktop to do the next very important stage of making a Swiss roll. Sprinkle the 2 tbsp caster sugar over the sponge while it is still hot. Put another

cont...

sheet of baking parchment over the sponge and, grabbing each side of the still-hot tin with your oven gloves, flip it over quickly. Remove the tin and leave the sponge to cool for 5 minutes, still covered on both sides with baking parchment.

For the filling, in a bowl or stand mixer, beat the vegan margarine with the icing sugar, then add the sour cherries. Combine until you have a fluffy pink cream.

Remove the top sheet of baking parchment from the fairly cool sponge. Spread the filling, using a rubber spatula or a palette knife, over the sponge. Then, starting from the short end and using the bottom layer of parchment to aid you, carefully roll up the sponge and cream layer into a roulade shape. Imagine you are rolling sushi! Still in its parchment, wrap the Swiss roll tightly in clingfilm and chill in the fridge until ready to use.

To make the jelly, put all the ingredients in a medium saucepan and bring to the boil. Simmer for 5 minutes, then take off the heat and let it cool. It's important not to use too much agar agar powder or it will set too hard and have an unpleasant mouthfeel; better to have slightly less than more, and every brand has its own strength, so it's hard to see until it sets whether it has gelled or not.

To assemble, remove the Swiss roll from the fridge and take off the clingfilm. Using a sharp knife, slice the roll into 1.5cm slices. Line the bottom and the sides of a glass dish with the slices. Then fill the bottom with a layer of morello or black cherries. Pour in the cooled jelly to cover the cake and cherries, leaving space on top for the cream, and put it in the fridge to set (you may not need all the jelly, depending on the size of your trifle dish).

Once the jelly has set, either squirt or pipe thick vegan cream onto the jelly, dotting it around the edge and the centre. Add the fresh cherries, stems up. Dust with icing sugar and serve.

Slow-Roasted Strawberries with Crunchy Bars & Raspberry Powder

Serves 6—8

This is a kind of alternative Eton mess with honeycomb rather than meringue. For this you will need a digital thermometer, which I recommend all cooks should buy anyway. You can get one for around £15. That's unless you know your stuff when it comes to sugar and can tell by the water method — dropping a little of the boiling sugar into a glass of water and seeing if it solidifies.

400g strawberries

100g sugar

1 tin of soya whipped cream or Thick Soya Cream (see page 30)

2 tbsp freeze-dried raspberry powder (available from some supermarkets and online)

For the honeycomb:

4 tbsp golden syrup

200g caster sugar

1 tbsp bicarbonate of soda

Preheat the oven to 160°C/gas mark 2½.

Pick the leaves off the strawberries, leaving the stalks. Line a baking tray with a silicone baking mat or a sheet of baking parchment. Spread the strawberries out, sprinkle over the sugar and roast for 30 minutes. Let cool and reserve the syrup.

Line a baking tin, around 20cm square, with baking parchment or foil.

Put the syrup and sugar in a medium saucepan over a high heat, and stir occasionally until it reaches 150°C (the hard crack stage). Then, working quickly, add the bicarbonate of soda and pour it all into the prepared baking tin. Leave to cool, then cut the honeycomb into 5cm sections and remove from the tin.

Assemble the pudding just before serving, on a plate or in a glass for each person. Add layers of strawberries and syrup, honeycomb and whipped or thick soya cream, in that order. Sprinkle the freeze-dried raspberry powder on top and serve.

Roast Persimmons with Coconut Tapioca Pudding

Serves 6—8

Tapioca is a love or hate food, probably because of school dinners. I, for one, like the pearl-like texture of tapioca pudding. Tapioca is a starch. It isn't a form of pasta, like semolina, but from the cassava root. It has virtually no nutritional value whatsoever!

For the tapioca:

400ml boiling water

300g tapioca pearls

400ml tin of coconut milk

100g caster sugar

Pinch of sea salt

For the roast persimmons:

100g palm sugar, plus
    extra shavings to serve
    (optional)

100ml boiling water

4 persimmons

3 star anise

Thumb of ginger, peeled and
    finely grated

1 cinnamon stick

Preheat the oven to 200°C/gas mark 6.

Pour the boiling water into a saucepan and add the tapioca pearls. Cook for 5 minutes over a medium heat, stirring constantly, then add the coconut milk, caster sugar and salt. Cook over a low heat for another 10 minutes. Keep stirring, as it sticks easily. When the tapioca pearls are translucent, they are cooked.

For the persimmons, put the palm sugar and boiling water in a saucepan and stir over a low-medium heat until the sugar melts, to make a 1:1 syrup.

Cut the persimmons in half or into slices and place in a baking tin. Add the star anise, ginger and cinnamon stick to the tin. Pour over the syrup and roast in the hot oven for 10—15 minutes or until the edges are starting to caramelise.

With the tapioca still warm (it can also be served cold), portion it out into glasses, cups or small bowls, adding half a persimmon or a few slices on top of the tapioca. Add shavings of palm sugar to the top, if you like.

Summer Pudding with Stem Ginger, Lime & Coconut Cream

Serves 6—8

850g berries (blackcurrants, raspberries, strawberries cut in half, blueberries), washed and de-stemmed as appropriate

200g caster sugar

2—3 nubs of stem ginger in syrup, thinly sliced

1 tbsp coconut oil or vegan spread

8—10 slices of day-old thin, white, crustless bread

To garnish:

Mint leaves

Cornflowers or borage flowers

To serve:

Coconut Whipped Cream (see page 30)

Finely grated zest of 1 lime

Equipment:

1-litre pudding bowl, or Mason Cash pudding bowl in size 30

This recipe doesn't need any change to become vegan. It's a British summer classic and easy to make. You'll need a litre pudding basin for this (size 30 if you are using Mason Cash pudding bowls). Do make sure the bread is stale, as it will hold the pudding together better. Only unmould just before serving.

Put all the fruit, sugar and stem ginger in a large, heavy-bottomed saucepan and simmer over a low-medium heat for 5—10 minutes until all the sugar has dissolved. Then remove from the heat and set aside. Once cool, drain off some of the juice into a shallow dish.

Grease a 1-litre pudding basin with the coconut oil or vegan spread. Dip the slices of bread into the juice and use to line the sides and base of the pudding basin. If you run out of juice, drain off some more from the fruit.

Spoon the fruit into the bread-lined basin, then add more slices of bread to cover the top, so that all the fruit is encased. Then place a saucer (which fits inside the rim) over the bread and a can of food or weight on top of the saucer. Chill in the fridge for at least a couple of hours.

To serve, dip the bowl briefly into hot water, then flip it over onto a serving plate and lift off the basin. Garnish with mint leaves and cornflowers or borage flowers. Serve with Coconut Whipped Cream mixed with the lime zest.

Selection Box of Raw Chocolates

Makes approximately 12 chocolates

100g cocoa butter, chopped

3–4 tbsp cacao powder

½ tsp finely ground sea salt

4 tbsp agave nectar or brown rice syrup, or 100g caster sugar

Flavouring options:

Finely grated lemon or orange zest

Lavender sugar

Ras el hanout spice mix (decorate with a rose petal)

Chopped nuts: hazelnuts, walnuts, pecan nuts, almonds

Decoration options:

Crystallised violets

Rose petals

Silver or gold leaf

Glitter or other cake decorations

Equipment:

Chocolate mould or flexible ice-cube mould

I suggest you buy a chocolate mould for these — available very cheaply at Lakeland — or use a flexible, bendy ice-cube mould. Once the ingredients are melted down, the mixture is liquid and therefore you need to pour it into a mould, then chill it until set.

Do not confuse cocoa and cacao! Cacao is raw, unroasted cocoa beans, which are the dried and fermented beans you find in the cacao fruit, from which all chocolate comes. The rest of the fruit tastes rather like custard apple. Cocoa is the roasted version of the ground-up beans which releases the oils and the 'butter'. (Photo on page 164.)

Put the cocoa butter in a heatproof bowl and set the bowl over a pan of boiling water so that the bottom of the bowl is not touching the water. Melt, then add the cacao powder, salt and agave nectar, syrup or sugar.

If not using flavourings, pour into your clean, dry mould, put straight into the fridge or freezer and leave to cool for a couple of hours. Then pop the chocolates out from the mould.

If using flavourings, decant the melted mixture into bowls and add the flavourings, taking care that the mixture doesn't start to cool. Then pour into the mould.

If using decorations, either pop them into the bottom of the mould or dab them onto the finished chocolate at the end with a touch of melted chocolate.

Variation: If you add a little nut milk and sweetener, you will end up with a thick chocolate paste that will set less hard. Once cooled, you can roll this into small balls and then roll in cocoa powder to make truffles.

Fleur de Sel Chocolate Peanut Butter Cups with Popping Candy

Serves 6

You need a silicone cupcake tray for this recipe. This way you can 'paint' the chocolate inside, then peel off the insides.

- 200g vegan dark chocolate, broken into pieces
- 2 tbsp vegetable shortening, such as Trex
- 200g smooth peanut butter
- 300g icing sugar
- 3 tbsp virgin coconut oil
- 1 tsp pure vanilla extract
- 1 tsp fleur de sel or other good-quality sea salt
- 75g popping candy

Equipment:
Silicone cupcake tray

Put the chocolate and shortening in a bowl and melt in the microwave for 30 seconds. Take it out, give it a stir and then microwave for another 30 seconds. If it needs a little more time, stick it in for another 30 seconds. Do not do it for longer bursts or it will ruin (or 'seize') the chocolate. Set aside some of the mixture, to cover the tops.

Then with a clean, dry pastry brush, paint the insides of a silicone cupcake tray with the melted chocolate. Paint it quite thickly, leaving it to dry, then paint a second layer. (You want it fairly thick so that you can release it from the silicone without it breaking.) Put it in the fridge to set.

Combine the peanut butter, icing sugar, coconut oil, vanilla and salt in a medium saucepan. Heat gently over a low heat until melted, then whip together with a whisk or rubber spatula until smooth. You don't want it too hot.

Remove the chocolate-lined silicone tray from the fridge and scoop 1 tbsp of the peanut butter mixture into each hole to reach just below the top. Then smooth it over. Leave to chill in the fridge while you prepare the next stage.

Heat the reserved chocolate in a bowl set over a pan of simmering water, or give it 15 seconds in the microwave. Then add the popping candy. Paint or spoon the mixture carefully over the top of your peanut butter cups. Chill once more in the fridge for about 10–15 minutes or until set.

Remove the tray from the fridge and, using your thumbnail, release each peanut butter cup round the sides from the silicone. Gently pull away the silicone and push up from the bottom to remove each cup.

Index

Acknowledgements

This book came about because of a vegan supper club collaboration between myself and Terry Hope Romero. I was talking about how successful it was to Ed Griffiths, head of publicity at Quadrille, and this is the result! So thank you to both Terry and Ed.

I'd like to thank Carolyn Stapleton of Black Cat (vegan) café, formerly the infamous anarchist vegan co-op Pogo café, in Clapton for her advice.

Thanks to my vegan testers:
Monica Shaw of Smarter Fitter, Gloria Nicol of The Laundry, Lucy Pearson, Josie Price, Lisa Roberjot, Michelle Eshkeri of Lavender Bakery, Linda Mazure, Diana McAllister, Carolyn Stapleton.

Thanks to my agent Michael Alcock.

Thanks to Catherine Phipps for her words of wisdom during the lonely process of writing a book.

Thanks to the brave and visionary team at Quadrille for commissioning this beauty of a book: Jane O'Shea, Helen Lewis, editor Céline Hughes, Simon Davis, designer Anita Mangan, food stylist Alice Hart (and her assistant), prop master David Herbert and photographer Jan Baldwin.

To my dad, John Rodgers, who has recently come to learn the benefits of a vegan diet

First published in 2015 by Quadrille Publishing Limited

Text © Kerstin Rodgers 2015
Photography © Jan Baldwin 2015

Quadrille is an imprint of Hardie Grant
www.hardiegrant.com.au

Quadrille Publishing Limited
Pentagon House
52–54 Southwark Street
London SE1 1UN
www.quadrille.co.uk

ISBN 978 184949 5035

British Library Cataloguing-in-Publication Data. A catalogue record for this book is available from the British Library.

Publishing Director: Jane O'Shea
Creative Director: Helen Lewis
Art Director/Designer: Anita Mangan
Photographer: Jan Baldwin
Food Stylist: Alice Hart
Props Stylist: David Herbert
Production: Stephen Lang and Vincent Smith

Printed and bound in China

www.cooked.com